Off The Grid
Preppers Food Survival Plan

*The Complete Step-by-Step DIY Guide to
Long-Term Food Security & Self-Sufficiency*

By

Andrew Raines

© Copyright 2024 - Andrew Raines

All rights reserved.

The content contained within this book may not be reproduced, duplicated or transmitted without direct written permission from the author or the publisher.

Under no circumstances will any blame or legal responsibility be held against the publisher, or author, for any damages, reparation, or monetary loss due to the information contained within this book, either directly or indirectly.

Legal Notice:

This book is copyright protected. It is only for personal use. You cannot amend, distribute, sell, use, quote or paraphrase any part, or the content within this book, without the consent of the author or publisher.

Disclaimer Notice:

Please note the information contained within this document is for educational and entertainment purposes only. All effort has been executed to present accurate, up to date, reliable, complete information. No warranties of any kind are declared or implied.

Readers acknowledge that the author is not engaged in the rendering of legal, financial, medical or professional advice. The content within this book has been derived from various sources. Please consult a licensed professional before attempting any techniques outlined in this book.

By reading this document, the reader agrees that under no circumstances is the author responsible for any losses, direct or indirect, th incurred as a result of the use of the information contained within this document, including, but not limited to, errors, omissions, or inaccuracies.

Contents

Introduction	1
1. Setting Goals & Building A Plan	3
2. Nutrition and Diet	11
3. Food Sources	46
4. DIY Food Preservation	57
5. Essential Foods	132
6. Stockpile and Pantry	151
7. Calculating Food Storage	173
8. Step-by-Step Stockpile Build	198
9. Meal Planning	207
10. Real World Examples	232
11. Plan Review and Checklist	237
Conclusion	241
Appendix A	243

INTRODUCTION

"In times of crisis, the most valuable currency is a full pantry."

In an uncertain world, having a reliable food supply is fundamental. Whether you're gearing up for emergencies, navigating economic fluctuations, or just aiming for a more self-sufficient way of living, this book is your go-to guide for confidently meeting your family's nutritional needs.

"*Off The Grid Prepper's Food Survival Plan*" combines practical advice with a touch of precision from my engineering background, making navigating the sometimes overwhelming world of long-term food survival easier. You'll discover how to pinpoint your essential foods, manage your stockpile, master food preservation techniques, and precisely calculate your household's needs.

Each chapter is designed for easy navigation, featuring straightforward steps, helpful tables, and bullet points to keep things clear. Plus, at the end of every chapter, you'll find a handy summary of key points that highlight critical information, along with a list of online resources with links to some great information on the web.

To assist you, I've created the *Prepper's Food Survival Calculator* which accurately determines the quantities of food you will need for your long-term storage. It's included in a free downloadable spreadsheet that features templates and blank tables to help you effectively plan your long-term food storage.

This book is about being accurate yet flexible to create a *Food Survival Plan* that suits your current needs and adapts as they change. By the time you finish, you'll have everything you need to set up a solid food storage system that keeps your family well-fed, no matter what life throws at you.

1

SETTING GOALS & BUILDING A PLAN

"Give me six hours to chop down a tree, and I will spend the first four sharpening the ax." Abraham Lincoln

Abe Lincoln nailed it when he used the tree chopping analogy. Planning and preparation are key – you can't chop down a tree with a dull axe!

Whether you're gearing up for a natural disaster, bracing for an economic slump, or just looking to live a more self-sufficient life, the first step is clear: define your goals and whip up a solid, actionable plan. Without that groundwork, even the best-stocked pantry won't cut it when you really need it.

Why Goals Matter

Goals give your *Food Survival Plan* meaning. They determine what you'll prioritize, how you'll structure your food storage, and which strategies will work best for you. Here are some common goals to consider as you begin:

Emergency Preparedness: Want to be ready for natural disasters, economic disruptions, or supply chain issues? Your plan will focus on a solid reserve of shelf-stable foods lasting 3–12 months.

Self-Sufficiency: Would you prefer to rely less on grocery stores? You'll prioritize homegrown and home-preserved foods, emphasizing independence.

Nutritional Balance: If health is your focus, you'll aim for a well-rounded stockpile that supports long-term wellness with various macronutrients and micronutrients.

Cost Efficiency: Are you tight on budget? You'll focus on stretching your dollars with strategic bulk purchases and cost-effective preservation methods.

These goals may evolve, and that's okay. The key is to start with a clear direction and adjust as needed.

The Importance of a Food Survival Plan

Imagine assembling a puzzle without knowing what the final image looks like. That's what food prepping without a plan feels like. A solid *Food Survival Plan* provides direction and purpose. It helps you make informed decisions about what to store, how much, and how to maintain a balanced diet, even in the most challenging times.

Your plan is your safety net. It ensures that you and your family have access to nutritious, satisfying meals no matter what challenges arise. But more than that, it empowers you to face uncertainty with confidence and peace of mind.

Plan Overview

This book is designed to take you step-by-step through creating a comprehensive, long-term *Food Survival Plan*. Each chapter builds on the last, giving you the tools and knowledge to achieve food security and self-sufficiency. Let's take a brief look at what's ahead:

Nutrition and Diet

A survival plan isn't just about stockpiling calories. It's about ensuring a balanced diet that provides all the nutrients your body needs to stay healthy and strong. This chapter will cover the basics of macronutrients and micronutrients and dietary considerations for different age groups and health conditions:

Nutritional Needs: The right mix of Carbs, Proteins, Fats & Oils, Fruit & Veg and Dairy.

Caloric Needs: Have enough calories to stay energized and healthy.

Superfoods: Boost the nutrition in your diet.

Impact of Preservation Methods: How they affect nutrient content.

Taste and Comfort Foods: Foods that contribute to positive mood and morale.

Food Sources

Where will your food come from? We'll explore various options, including grocery stores, farmers' markets, home gardens, and foraging. Some of your food sources will become the basis for your DIY food preservation:

Fresh Food: Great for nutrients but only lasts for a short time.

Canned Foods: Convenient and long-lasting, no need for refrigeration.

Dry Foods: Grains, legumes, and more with a long shelf life.

Store-bought Long-Life Foods: These are made to last long, making them convenient for preppers who want easy-to-store, ready-to-eat options.

DIY Preserved Food: Canned, Dehydrated, and Freeze-Dried items keep well and keep their nutrition.

DIY Food Preservation

Preserving your own food is a cornerstone of self-sufficiency. This chapter will provide step-by-step instructions for common methods like Canning, Dehydrating, and Fermenting, along with tips for maintaining food quality and safety:

DIY vs. Store-Bought: DIY food preservation saves money and encourages self-sufficiency but takes time and effort. Store-bought foods provide convenience and variety but can be pricey.

Picking the Best Preservation Method: Your fresh foods, dietary habits, and taste preferences will guide you in selecting the perfect DIY food preservation methods.

For Beginners: Start simple, invest wisely, preserve in batches, learn from others, keep track of costs, and stay organized.

Seasonal Planning: Planning ahead ensures you have a variety of tasty and nutritious foods all year round, making you more resilient and self-sufficient.

Essential Foods

Not all foods are created equal when it comes to long-term storage and nutritional value. We'll identify the must-have items for your stockpile, from staples like rice and beans to versatile ingredients that add flavor and variety to your meals:

Nutrition and Calories: Important to eat healthy and maintain energy.

Food Groups: Include a good variety from the five major food groups.

Preserved Foods: A mix of store-bought and DIY preserved foods.

Taste and Comfort: Foods that contribute to positive mood and morale.

Your Essential Food List: The basis for your long-term stored food.

Non-Food Items: Valuable items to include for the long term.

Stockpile and Pantry

Organization is key to maintaining a functional food supply. Learn how to build and maintain a well-organized pantry, rotate your stockpile, and avoid waste:

Optimize Storage Conditions: Keep your stockpile and pantry neat and organized to keep your food fresh and safe.

Storage in Small Spaces: Be creative and stay organized for small spaces.

Waterproofing Food Storage: To prevent moisture-related spoilage, mold, and contamination.

Food Storage Containers: Store your food correctly to keep it fresh and safe by choosing suitable food containers.

3-Tier Food Storage Method: Store foods in Short (Tier 1), Intermediate (Tier 2), and Long-term (Tier 3) categories for easy access and maintenance.

FIFO Step-by-Step: Follow the steps to implement the First-in, First-out method to organize and rotate your foods.

Calculating Food Storage

How much food do you really need? Download the free spreadsheet and use the exclusive Prepper's Food Survival Calculator to quickly determine how much food you need to keep your family fed and healthy.

Household: Use the spreadsheet to calculate the caloric food needs for your family.

Prepper's Food Survival Calculator: Use the calculator to determine your household food storage quantities using the Caloric or Serving-Based methods.

LDS Calculator: Use the original LDS Food Storage Calculator for bulk food quantities. The Amended LDS Calculator substitutes fresh foods for preserved foods and rebalances the food groups to meet accepted guidelines.

Step-by-Step Stockpile Build

Putting it all together, we'll walk you through the process of building your stockpile. From budgeting to shopping to storage, you'll gain practical tips for turning your plan into reality.

Step-by-Step Stockpile Build: Follow the steps to build your own stockpile.

Start Small: Slowly build up your stockpile.

Stockpile on a Budget: Create solid food storage without spending a fortune.

Meal Planning

A stockpile is only helpful if you know how to use it. Discover strategies for planning nutritious, delicious meals that are easy to prepare with your stored ingredients:

7-Day & 30-Day Meal Plans: Complete your 7-day & 30-day Meal Plans using the table templates.

Emergency Meal Planning: Use the 3-Tier food storage method to help develop plans for different emergency scenarios

Emergency Meal Kit: Follow the step-by-step guide to build your Meal Kit for short-term emergencies.

Real-World Examples

Get inspired by real-life stories of individuals and families who successfully implement food survival plans. Learn from their successes and challenges as you refine your own approach.

Plan Review and Checklist

Building a plan is just the beginning; keeping it effective requires regular review and maintenance. In this chapter, you'll learn how to evaluate your stockpile's condition, update your plan as your needs change, and ensure your food supply stays fresh, organized, and ready to use.

Lastly, go through the *Food Survival Plan Checklist* to ensure everything is covered.

Wrapping it Up...

Creating a *Food Survival Plan* can feel overwhelming, especially starting from scratch. But remember: every step you take brings you closer to your goal. Begin by setting clear, achievable objectives, and use this book as your guide. When you reach the final chapter, you'll have a personalized plan that gives you the confidence to face the future.

Let's get started.

2

NUTRITION AND DIET

Your brain uses about 20% of your daily calorie intake, even when you're just thinking

When putting together a long-term *Food Survival Plan*, nailing down your nutrition and diet is important for keeping everyone healthy, energized, and ready to face whatever life throws at you. Sure, stockpiling food is essential, but ensuring that what you have meets your family's nutritional needs is just as crucial.

In this chapter, we'll learn how to balance calories, macronutrients, and micronutrients while focusing on preserved and shelf-stable options. We'll cover everything from picking nutrient-dense superfoods, figuring out each family member's caloric needs, and adding some comfort foods to keep everyone's spirits up. By the end, you'll have a solid understanding of the role of nutrition and diet in crafting your own *Food Survival Plan*.

Macronutrients

Macronutrients are the crucial nutrients your body needs in significant quantities to work well. They consist of carbohydrates, proteins, and fats, each serving an essential purpose in keeping you healthy and energized. Understanding macronutrients is vital for creating a balanced and sustainable long-term food storage for preppers.

Carbohydrates

Carbohydrates are your body's primary energy source, giving you the fuel you need for everyday activities and keeping everything running smoothly. They're especially crucial for your brain and help you stay energized during physical activities.

Key Foods

Grains: Whole grains like rice, oats, wheat, and cornmeal should form the backbone of your carbohydrate stores. These staples have a long shelf life and can be used in various meals.

Legumes: Beans, lentils, and peas are good protein sources and complex carbohydrates. They can be dried and stored for extended periods, offering energy and nutrients.

Root Vegetables (Dehydrated): Potatoes, sweet potatoes, and carrots can be dehydrated and stored as an additional source of carbohydrates. These provide essential vitamins and minerals along with energy.

Proteins

Proteins are vital in building and repairing tissues, producing enzymes and hormones, and boosting immune health. Having enough protein on hand is crucial for staying strong and healthy.

Key Foods

Legumes: Dried beans, lentils, and chickpeas are excellent plant-based protein sources. They are nutrient-dense, long-lasting, and versatile in cooking.

Canned Meats: Store canned chicken, tuna, salmon, and other meats as reliable protein sources that do not require refrigeration.

Nuts and Seeds: Almonds, peanuts, sunflower seeds, and other nuts and seeds are compact, calorie-dense protein sources.

Fats and Oils

Fats and oils are essential for brain health, hormone production, and the absorption of fat-soluble vitamins (A, D, E, and K). They also provide a concentrated energy source, which is crucial for survival.

Key Foods

Oils: Olive, coconut, and vegetable oils are vital for cooking and adding healthy fats to your diet.

Nuts and Seeds: Besides being protein sources, nuts and seeds are rich in healthy fats. They can be eaten as snacks or used in cooking to boost caloric intake.

Fatty Fish: Options like sardines, mackerel, and salmon are rich in omega-3 fatty acids, which are essential for heart health and cognitive function. These also provide a good balance of protein and fats.

Fruits and Vegetables

While not directly categorized under macronutrients, fruits and vegetables provide essential vitamins, minerals, and fiber, contributing to overall health.

Key Foods

Dehydrated and Freeze-Dried: Fruits and Vegetables retain most of their nutritional value and have a long shelf life.

Canned Vegetables: These are a convenient and reliable source of nutrients. Look for low-sodium options and rotate stock regularly to maintain freshness.

Dairy

Dairy products and their alternatives offer additional sources of protein and fats.

Key Foods

Powdered Milk and Cheese: These are excellent for long-term storage and can be used in various recipes.

Shelf-Stable Milk and Cheese: This includes long-lasting milk options like Ultra-High Temperature (UHT) milk, evaporated and condensed milk, and processed and canned cheese.

Building a Balanced Food Storage

When putting together your long-term food storage, you must create a well-rounded selection of carbs, proteins, fats, fruits & vegs, dairy, and other must-haves, focusing on durability and packed with nutrients. Here is a balanced food group ratio you can use for long-term food storage:

Carbohydrates	30-40%
Proteins	15-25%
Fats & Oils	15-20%
Fruits and Vegetables	15-20%
Dairy	10-15%

Micronutrients

While macronutrients are essential for energy and building our bodies, we can't overlook micronutrients, those crucial vitamins and minerals that keep us healthy. Even though we need them in smaller amounts, they're critical for immune support, bone health, and fighting off chronic diseases. So, having a good stash of these micronutrients is crucial, especially when relying on your food supply.

Micronutrients break down into two main types

Vitamins: These organic compounds help with energy production, immune function, and cell repair.

Minerals: These are inorganic elements that aid in bone formation, fluid balance, and nerve function.

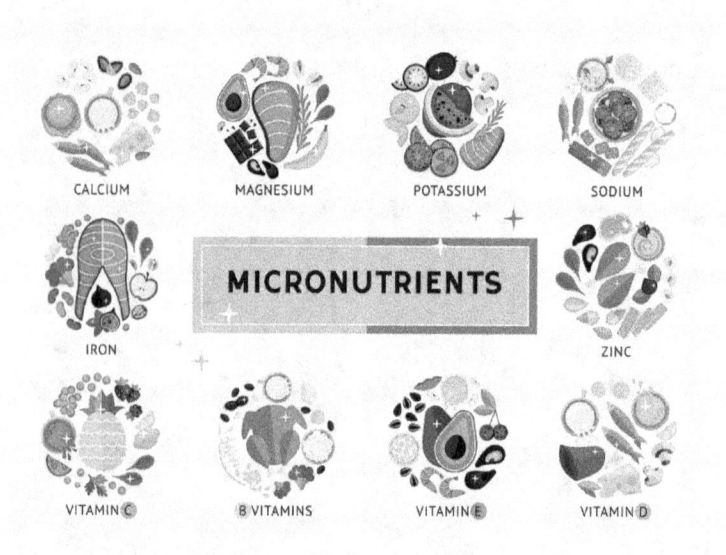

Key Vitamins and Minerals

Getting enough vitamins and minerals can damage your health and cause weak immunity, fatigue, and slow healing. If you're relying on preserved foods, here are the essentials to keep an eye on:

Vitamin A: Great for your eyes and skin. Find it in dried apricots and carrots.

Vitamin C: Boosts immunity and skin health. Look for it in dried fruits and sauerkraut.

Vitamin D: Important for bones and immunity. Sunlight is best, but supplements help, too.

Vitamin E: An antioxidant found in nuts and seeds.

B-Vitamins: Key for energy and brain function. Get them from fortified cereals and whole grains.

Calcium: Essential for bones and muscles. Think powdered milk and fortified plant milk.

Iron: Crucial for oxygen transport. Canned meats and beans are good sources.

Zinc: Supports immunity and healing. Find it in nuts and seeds.

Food Storage Tips

To keep your food stash nutritionally balanced:

Mix It Up: Stock a variety of foods to cover all your micronutrient bases. Canned, dried, and freeze-dried fruits and veggies are great options.

Fortified Foods: Grab some fortified cereals and plant-based milks to fill gaps.

Supplements: Keep some multivitamins handy for emergencies, and consider specific ones like vitamin D or iron if you need them.

Check Expiration Dates: Store supplements in a cool, dry place and monitor their shelf life.

> **Key Takeaway**
>
> Both macronutrients and micronutrients are essential for staying healthy in the long run, especially regarding food storage. Macronutrients give your body the energy and structure it needs. At the same time, micronutrients play a crucial role in keeping your immune system strong, your bones healthy, and your overall well-being in check. Having a well-rounded stash of nutrient-dense foods and a solid plan is essential to avoid deficiencies and stay strong during times of self-reliance.

Preserved Foods

Stocking up on preserved foods is smart for keeping your nutrition on point, especially when fresh stuff is hard to find. Canning, dehydrating, and freeze-drying do a great job of keeping the good stuff, like vitamins and minerals, intact. They're perfect for emergencies or when you want to be self-sufficient. Plus, they help you mix your meals with proteins, carbs, and fats so you stay healthy and energized. A variety of preserved foods can keep your meals tasty and exciting.

In the next chapter, we'll examine preserved foods in more detail, with step-by-step guides to all common DIY food preservation methods.

Nutrition in Preserved Foods

Preserving foods can affect nutrient content. For example, while methods like Freezing, Dehydration, and Canning extend shelf life, they may reduce some vitamins and minerals, especially heat-sensitive ones like vitamins C and B. Each method has its own impact on nutrients. Freezing is good for keeping most of them. Dehydration is excellent for fiber and carbs, and Pressure

Canning helps maintain protein and fiber. Understanding how these methods affect nutrients can help you ensure you're still getting all the good stuff you need from preserved foods.

To maximize nutritional value

Variety: Use a combination of preserved foods to ensure a wide range of nutrients. Different foods and preservation methods can complement each other nutritionally.

Rotation: Regularly rotate your stock of preserved foods to use the oldest items first, ensuring that your food supply remains as nutritious as possible.

Supplement Fresh Foods: Whenever possible, supplement your preserved food supply with fresh produce to boost your intake of vitamins and minerals.

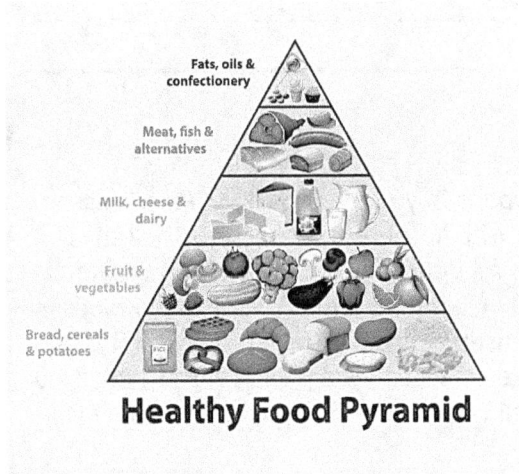

Healthy Food Pyramid

This table summarizes the impact on nutrition of each food preservation method:

	Nutritional Impact	Key Points
Water Bath Canning	Vitamin C & B loss	High-acid foods, kills bacteria,
Pressure Canning	Protein retention	Low-acid foods, kills Clostridium botulinum spores
Dehydration	Concentrated nutrients, some vitamin loss	Lightweight, long shelf life, retains most nutrients.
Fermentation	Enhanced nutrients, adds probiotics	Increases nutrient availability, beneficial for gut health.
Freezing	Minimal nutrient loss	Best for preserving most vitamins and minerals.
Freeze-Drying	Minimal nutrient loss	Best for retaining most nutrients, long shelf life.
Vacuum Sealing	Nutrient preservation	Extends shelf life, maintains nutritional content when combined with freezing.
Pickling	Retains nutrients, adds probiotics	Adds flavor, High salt content, beneficial for gut health
Salting/Curing	Retains minerals, potential vitamin loss	High sodium content, long shelf life.
Sugaring	Retains vitamins, increases calories	High sugar content, good for fruits and preserves.
Smoking	Retains most nutrients, potential carcinogens	Adds flavor, may introduce harmful compounds.

Key Takeaway

Having preserved foods in your *Food Survival Plan* is essential. They're packed with nutrients that keep you healthy and feeling good. Knowing how different preservation methods affect nutrition and including a variety of preserved foods in your diet, you can ensure you're getting all the vitamins and minerals you need, even when food is scarce. This helps you stay healthy and ready for any emergencies that come your way.

Superfoods (Nutrient-Rich)

When stocking up on food and planning meals, remember superfoods. They're packed with nutrients and can be a great addition to your diet, especially in emergencies. Foods like blueberries, spinach, quinoa, and almonds are full of vitamins and minerals that can help keep you healthy when fresh produce is hard to come by.

Key Superfoods

Here are some key superfoods with their preservation methods and shelf life:

	Nutritional Benefit	Preservation Method	Shelf Life
Beef Jerky	High in protein, iron, zinc	Dehydration Commercial	1-2 months 1-2 years
Berries	High in antioxidants, vitamins C and K, fiber	Freezing Water Bath Canning	12 months 12-18 months
Chia Seeds	High in omega-3 fatty acids, fiber, protein, calcium	Dehydration Vacuum Sealing	Up to 5 years
Cruciferous Vegetables	High in fiber, vitamins C and K, folate, antioxidants	Freezing Pickling	8-12 months 12 months
Dried Fruits	High in fiber, vitamins A and C, potassium	Dehydration Vacuum Sealing	12-18 months 12 months
Fish	Rich in omega-3 fatty acids, protein, vitamins D and B12	Pressure Canning Freezing	12-18 months 6-9 months
Flax Seeds	Omega-3 fatty acids, fiber	Dehydrated, Vacuum Sealed	Up to 1 year
Garlic	Immune-boosting properties	Fresh, Oil, Powdered	6 months - 1 year
Honey	Natural sweetener, antioxidant, antimicrobial	Dry Storage	Indefinite
Kale	Vitamins A, K, C	Dehydrated Powdered	6-12 months
Leafy Greens	Rich in vitamins A, C, K, folate, fiber	Freezing Dehydrating	8-12 months 6-12 months
Legumes	High in protein, fiber, iron, folate	Pressure Canning Dehydration	12-18 months 12 months
Nuts and Seeds	Good source of healthy fats, protein, fiber, vitamins E and B	Dehydration Vacuum Sealing	12 months 12-18 months
Quinoa	High in protein, fiber, iron, magnesium, complete protein	Vacuum Sealing Dry Storage	2-3 years 6-12 months

Preserving Superfoods

Picking the right ways to keep nutrient-packed foods fresh helps you keep all those good-for-you nutrients and maximize their health perks. Freezing, Freeze-Drying, Vacuum Sealing, and Fermentation are top methods for maintaining nutritious superfoods. By choosing the right preservation methods, you can enjoy the health advantages of these foods all year long.

This table highlights the nutrient retention of superfoods for different preservation methods:

	Nutrient Retention	Example Superfoods
Water Bath Canning	Good retention of fiber and some vitamins	Berries, Tomatoes, Pickles
Pressure Canning	Good retention of protein and fiber	Legumes, Fish, Meats
Dehydrating	Good retention of fiber and carbohydrates	Leafy Greens, Fruits, Herbs, Nuts and Seeds
Fermentation	Enhances probiotics and vitamin B, good retention of fiber	Cabbage (kimchi, sauerkraut), Cucumbers (pickles), Soybeans (miso, tempeh), Dairy (yogurt, kefir)
Freezing	High retention of vitamins and minerals	Berries, Leafy Greens, Cruciferous Vegetables, Fish
Freeze-Drying	Excellent retention of vitamins, minerals, and flavor	Berries, Fruits, Vegetables, Meats, Dairy
Vacuum Sealing	Excellent retention, especially when combined with freezing or drying	Whole Grains, Nuts and Seeds, Dried Fruits, Chia Seeds
Pickling	Good retention of fiber and some vitamins, adds probiotics	Cruciferous Vegetables, Cucumbers
Salting / Curing	Good retention of protein, adds sodium	Meats, Fish, Cheese
Sugaring	Good retention of fiber, adds sugars	Fruits, Ginger
Smoking	Good retention of protein, can lose some vitamins	Meats, Fish, Nuts

Calories

Calories are a measure of energy. They are essential for the body to perform basic functions such as breathing, circulating blood, and physical activities. The amount of energy provided by food is measured in calories. Here is a breakdown of the calories of common foods:

Carbohydrates: They typically range from 20 to 30 calories per ounce and include grains, fruits, vegetables, and legumes.

Proteins: Range from 30 to 50 calories per ounce: Includes meat, poultry, fish, eggs, dairy products, beans, and nuts.

Fats & Oils: Range from 200 to 250 calories per ounce: Includes oils, nuts, seeds, avocados, and fatty fish.

Comparing Fresh Food vs. Preserved Food

When comparing the calories of fresh and preserved foods, there are some important differences to remember. Fresh foods usually have fewer calories than preserved ones. This is because preserved foods often have extra sugars, salts, and fats added during the preservation process, which can bump up their calorie count.

Fresh Foods

Fruits: Fresh fruits like apples, berries, and oranges are naturally low in calories and high in water content.

Vegetables: Fresh vegetables such as carrots, spinach, and broccoli are low-calorie and nutrient-dense.

Meats: Fresh meats (chicken, beef, fish) are leaner and have fewer calories than processed versions.

Preserved Foods

Canned Fruits: Often contain added sugars, increasing their calorie content compared to fresh fruits.

Canned Vegetables: May have added salts and preservatives, slightly increasing their calorie count.

Dried Fruits: Higher calories due to the concentration of natural sugars and potential added sweeteners.

Canned Meats: Typically have added fats and preservatives, leading to higher calorie counts than fresh meats.

Processed Foods: Foods like jerky or smoked meats often have added salts and fats, making them more calorie-dense.

Preserved foods are handy, last longer, and have more calories. This can be an advantage when stockpiling food, as fewer quantities are required since the preserved food has a higher caloric density.

This table shows the calorie content of some common fresh foods and their preserved equivalent, including serving sizes and calorie counts:

Fresh Food & Serving Size	Calories	Preserved Equivalent	Calories	Notes
Beef (1 oz)	71	Canned Beef	90	Canning often includes additional fats or oils, increasing the calorie content slightly.
Beans (1 cup)	199	Canned Beans	210	Canned beans may have added salt or sugars, slightly increasing the calorie count.
Peaches (1 Cup)	37	Canned Peaches	100	Canned peaches are often packed in syrup, significantly increasing the sugar and calories.
Ham (3 oz)	110	Canned Ham	130	Canned ham may contain added preservatives and fats, leading to higher calorie content.
Apples (6 oz)	87	Dried Apples	480	Dried apples are more calorie-dense due to the removal of water, concentrating the sugars.
Apricots (¼ cup)	17	Dried Apricots	78	Similar to apples, drying apricots concentrates the sugars, increasing the calorie density.
Tomatoes (5 oz)	22	Canned Tomatoes	25	The calorie difference is minimal, but canned tomatoes may have slight variations due to added ingredients.
Strawberries (1 oz)	9	Freeze-Dried Strawberries	90	Freeze-drying removes water, concentrating the sugars and calories in the fruit.
Beets (6 oz)	44	Pickled Beets	110	Pickling often involves added sugars or syrups, leading to a higher calorie count.
Cucumbers (4 oz)	6	Pickles	20	Pickles are cucumbers preserved in brine, often with added sugars or salt, increasing the calories slightly.
Cod (3 oz)	71	Canned Cod	80	Canned cod may include added oils or brine, slightly increasing the calories.
Cabbage (1 cup)	58	Sauerkraut	70	The fermentation process slightly increases the calorie content in sauerkraut.
Salmon (3 oz)	177	Canned Salmon	118	Canned salmon typically has lower fat content, resulting in fewer calories compared to fresh salmon.

Caloric Needs

Calorie needs vary from person to person. Age, gender, muscle mass, and activity level all play a part. As we get older, our metabolism slows down, so we might not need as many calories as we used to. Generally, men need more calories than women because they usually have more muscle. If you're active, you'll need more fuel than someone who isn't. Life changes like stress, illness, or pregnancy can increase your calorie needs. So, when planning meals, remember all this to find what works best for you.

Average Calorie Requirements

Let's take a look at caloric requirements and what variables can affect how much you need. Here are the general caloric needs for adults and children:

Adults

Men: 2,200 to 3,000 calories per day

Women: 1,800 to 2,400 calories per day

Children

Toddlers (1-3 years):   1,000 to 1,400 calories per day

Preschoolers (4-5 years):   1,200 to 1,600 calories per day

School-aged (6-12 years):   1,400 to 2,200 calories per day

Teenagers (13-18 years):   1,800 to 2,800 calories per day

Key Variables

It's crucial to tweak these numbers based on factors affecting your energy requirements. Here are some specific adjustments to consider for various factors:

Age

- Caloric needs generally decrease with age due to a slower metabolism and reduced physical activity levels.
- Decrease by approximately 100-200 calories daily every decade after age 30.

Body Composition

- Individuals with more muscle mass have higher caloric needs since muscle tissue burns more calories than fat tissue, even at rest.
- Increase by 50-100 calories per 10 pounds of muscle gained.

Individual Metabolism

- Metabolic rates vary from person to person. Some individuals naturally burn more calories at rest than others.
- Metabolic rate can vary by about 100-300 calories per day based on individual differences.

Activity Level

- Individuals with higher activity levels burn more calories and thus require more food.
- Levels: Sedentary, Lightly Active, Moderately Active, Very Active, Extra Active
- Increase by 200-400 calories per level of activity above sedentary.

Health Status

- Illnesses, injuries, and medical conditions can affect caloric needs. For instance, recovering from surgery or fighting an infection can increase energy requirements.
- Increase by 100-300 calories per day for recovery periods.

Pregnancy and Breastfeeding

- Pregnant and breastfeeding women have higher caloric

needs to support fetal growth and milk production.

- Increase by 300-500 calories per day

> **Key Takeaway**
>
> Counting calories can be tricky because it involves some number crunching. Even if you're careful, many factors can throw off your calculations. Aiming for a balanced diet that matches your burning calories is important. If you start gaining or losing weight, the balance may be off. Also, remember that preserved foods have more calories than fresh ones.

Water in Nutrition and Diet

Water is crucial for keeping you hydrated and is key to your nutrition and diet. It's essential for many bodily functions that are necessary for staying healthy and feeling good:

Digestion: Water aids in the breakdown of food, allowing nutrients to be absorbed efficiently in the intestines.

Nutrient Transport: It facilitates the transport of vitamins, minerals, and other nutrients throughout the body via the bloodstream.

Metabolism: Water is necessary for metabolic processes that convert food into energy.

Detoxification: It helps remove waste products and toxins from the body through urine and sweat.

Temperature Regulation: Water helps maintain body temperature through sweating and respiration.

Water-Rich Foods

Incorporating water-rich foods into your diet can enhance hydration and provide essential nutrients. Here are a few water-rich foods to consider:

	Food	Water Content	Nutritional Benefits
Fruits	Watermelon	90%+	Vitamins A and C
	Strawberries	90%+	Antioxidants, Vitamin C
	Oranges	87%	Vitamin C, Fiber
Vegetables	Cucumbers	95%	Vitamins K and C
	Lettuce	95%	Low in calories, Vitamins A and K
	Zucchini	95%	Vitamins B6, C, and Potassium
Dairy/Alternatives	Milk	High	Calcium, Protein, Vitamins D and B12
	Yogurt	High	Protein, Probiotics, Calcium

Water Availability

Ensuring you have enough water is crucial for being prepared in an emergency. Here are some tips on how to make sure you have a reliable water supply and how to manage it effectively:

Storage: Store at least one gallon of water per person daily for at least two weeks. This includes water for drinking, cooking, and hygiene.

Rainwater Harvesting: Collect and store rainwater using rain barrels or other collection systems. Ensure proper filtration and purification before use.

Natural Sources: Identify and access local natural water sources such as rivers, lakes, and springs. Always treat or purify water from these sources before consumption.

Water Storage

Keeping enough water on hand is crucial for being prepared in an emergency. Here are some strategies for storing your water supply:

Containers

Commercial Options: Use large-capacity water barrels or tanks made of food-grade plastic with UV inhibitors.

Portable Containers: Smaller, portable containers are useful for transport and short-term storage.

DIY Solutions: Repurpose food-grade barrels and set up rainwater catchment systems for a renewable water source.

Storage Conditions

Location: Store water in a cool, dark place to prevent algae growth and container degradation.

Rotation: Rotate stored water every six months to maintain freshness.

Disinfection: Add unscented bleach (about eight drops per gallon) to keep water safe for drinking.

Purification Methods

Keeping your water quality in check is crucial for preventing illnesses and ensuring water safety. Here are some tips to help you maintain good water quality:

Boiling: For at least one minute (three minutes at higher altitudes) effectively kills bacteria, viruses, and parasites.

Chemical Purification: Use purification tablets or drops (chlorine, iodine) according to the package instructions.

Filtration: Portable water filters or household filtration systems can remove contaminants and improve taste. Ensure filters are rated for the types of pollutants present.

Solar Disinfection (SODIS): Expose clear plastic bottles filled with water to direct sunlight for at least six hours. UV rays can help kill pathogens.

Practical Tips

Regular Maintenance: Rotate stored water every six months to ensure freshness. Clean and sanitize storage containers before refilling.

Emergency Kits: Include water purification methods in your emergency kits, such as purification tablets, a portable filter, and a metal container for boiling water.

Water Conservation: To maximize your water supply, practice water conservation use water-efficient practices when cooking, cleaning, and bathing.

Water is crucial for staying alive and healthy, especially during emergencies. Ensuring you have clean drinking water is a big part of being prepared. Having a dependable water supply and keeping it clean can help you stay healthy and happy. Plus, it ties into maintaining a good diet and nutrition plan no matter the situation.

If you're looking for practical tips on how to find, purify, and store water, check out *Prepper's Water Survival Plan*, another book in the *Off The Grid* survival series. It's packed with useful information.

https://mybook.to/BIWnfTB

Taste and Comfort Foods

While staples like grains, proteins, and canned goods are crucial for long-term survival, a well-rounded food stockpile should include more than just the basics. Adding herbs, spices, condiments, comfort foods, and beverages to your supplies is important for making your meals practical and enjoyable over time. These extras amp up the flavor and help with your emotional well-being, making challenging situations easier to handle. Here's why these items are must-haves for any prepper's food list, along with some handy examples:

Herbs and Spices

Herbs and spices are powerful and versatile ingredients that significantly enhance your meals' flavor, nutritional value, and health benefits, especially in a prepper's food stockpile. Often overlooked in emergency preparedness, these small but impactful items can significantly improve the taste and healthiness of your stored foods. By including a variety of herbs and spices in your prepper's pantry, you can make your meals more enjoyable and provide extra health benefits, which can be essential during long periods of self-sufficiency.

Enhancing Flavor and Variety

One of the most critical roles of herbs and spices is to transform basic, often repetitive meals into flavorful and enjoyable dishes. In a survival scenario where your diet may consist of simple staples like rice, beans, canned goods, herbs and spices, you can prevent food fatigue by adding diverse and vibrant flavors.

Food Preservation Qualities

Beyond flavor, many herbs and spices have natural preservative properties that make them valuable for long-term food storage.

These preservation qualities can help extend the shelf life of your food and ensure that it remains safe to eat:

Antimicrobial Properties: Herbs like garlic and onion contain compounds with natural antimicrobial effects, which can help inhibit the growth of bacteria and fungi, thereby preserving the freshness of your stored foods.

Antioxidants: Spices such as oregano and thyme are rich in antioxidants, which help prevent oxidation. This process can lead to food spoilage and nutrient loss. Including these spices in your meals can also help protect your food from the damaging effects of oxygen exposure.

Natural Preservatives: Turmeric, known for its vibrant yellow color, contains curcumin, a compound with strong antibacterial and antifungal properties. It's often used in preserving foods, particularly with salt and other methods.

Medicinal Benefits

In addition to their culinary and preservative roles, many herbs and spices offer significant medicinal benefits that can be particularly valuable in survival situations:

Immune Support: Garlic is renowned for its immune-boosting properties due to its high content of allicin, a compound that helps fight infections. Ginger is another powerful immune booster known for its anti-inflammatory and antioxidant effects.

Digestive Health: Ginger and peppermint are commonly used to alleviate digestive issues such as nausea, bloating, and indigestion. Fennel seeds are effective in reducing gas and supporting digestive comfort.

Anti-Inflammatory Effects: Turmeric is widely recognized for its anti-inflammatory properties, making it beneficial for managing chronic inflammation and pain. Cinnamon and cloves also have anti-inflammatory effects, which can help reduce pain and swelling.

Blood Sugar Regulation: Cinnamon has been shown to help regulate blood sugar levels by improving insulin sensitivity, making it particularly useful for people managing diabetes or pre-diabetes during a crisis.

Examples

Garlic Powder: A versatile spice that enhances the flavor of nearly any savory dish while offering immune-boosting benefits.

Cumin: Adds warmth and earthiness to dishes and aids in digestion.

Thyme: Versatile for soups, stews, and meats; also offers antioxidant and antimicrobial properties.

Oregano: A staple in Italian cooking that also acts as an antioxidant.

Cinnamon: For sweet and savory dishes, cinnamon has anti-inflammatory and blood sugar-regulating properties.

Turmeric: Adds color and flavor to foods while providing anti-inflammatory and antibacterial benefits.

Basil: Perfect for Italian dishes and rich in antioxidants, it has anti-inflammatory properties.

Peppermint: Great for soothing digestive issues and adding a fresh flavor to teas and desserts.

Condiments and Sauces

Condiments and sauces improve staple foods' taste, diversity, and nutritional content, making them vital for a comprehensive prepper's food supply. In addition to their cooking advantages, many condiments and sauces provide preservative properties and health benefits that can be especially useful in survival scenarios.

Enhancing Flavor and Variety

One of the main reasons to stock condiments and sauces in your prepper's pantry is their power to turn simple, often tasteless foods into delicious meals. In scenarios where your diet may become monotonous, the right condiments can help avoid food fatigue by providing a variety of flavors, from sweet and tangy to spicy and savory.

Food Preservation Qualities

Condiments and sauces do more than add flavor; many also contain natural preservatives that can prolong the shelf life of food, making them especially useful for long-term storage situations.

Vinegar-Based Sauces: Condiments like vinegar, mustard, and barbecue sauce are acidic, which inhibits the growth of bacteria and helps preserve foods. Vinegar is also commonly used in pickling, allowing you to preserve fresh vegetables for extended periods.

Salt Content: High-sodium condiments such as soy sauce and hot sauce act as preservatives by drawing moisture out of foods, which inhibits bacterial growth. This makes them useful not only for flavor but also for extending the shelf life of perishable items.

Oil-Based Sauces: Olive oil and other oil-based dressings can create a protective barrier on the foods' surface, helping preserve them. Olive oil is a staple in Mediterranean diets for cooking and preserving herbs and garlic.

Medicinal Benefits

In addition to their culinary and preservative roles, some condiments and sauces offer medicinal benefits that can support your health during emergencies:

Apple Cider Vinegar: Known for its digestive benefits, apple cider vinegar can help regulate stomach acidity and improve gut health, making it a valuable addition to your stockpile.

Capsaicin in Hot Sauce: The active compound in hot peppers, capsaicin, has anti-inflammatory and antimicrobial properties. It can also boost metabolism and provide pain relief by reducing the sensation of pain in the nervous system.

Probiotic Condiments: Fermented condiments like kimchi, sauerkraut, and some types of mustard contain beneficial bacteria (probiotics) that support digestive health and strengthen the immune system, which is crucial during stressful situations when access to fresh food might be limited.

Examples

Soy Sauce: A versatile condiment that adds umami flavor to various dishes and has preservative qualities due to its high salt content.

Vinegar (White, Apple Cider, Balsamic): It is useful for cooking, pickling, and as a base for dressings, and it has additional digestive benefits.

Hot Sauce: Adds heat and flavor while providing anti-inflammatory and antimicrobial benefits.

Ketchup and Mustard: Staple condiments that enhance the taste of many meals and offer preservative and antimicrobial properties in the case of mustard.

Olive Oil: A healthy fat used in cooking, dressings, and preserving foods, with the benefit of heart-healthy monounsaturated fats.

Barbecue Sauce: Ideal for adding a sweet and tangy flavor to meats, beans, and vegetables, with vinegar as a preservative.

Peanut Butter: Although more than a condiment, peanut butter is a versatile spread that adds protein and healthy fats to meals and snacks.

Comfort Foods

Comfort foods are typically seen as a luxury in daily life, but they become significantly more valuable in emergencies or long-term survival situations. Adding comfort foods to your food stockpile goes beyond satisfying cravings; it helps maintain morale, offers psychological relief, and creates a sense of normalcy during tough times. These foods can provide essential mental and emotional support for survival challenges.

Psychological Importance

Mood Enhancement: Comfort foods are associated with positive memories and emotional well-being. In stressful situations, consuming these foods can trigger the release of serotonin and endorphins—hormones that promote feelings of happiness and relaxation. For example, chocolate is well-known for its mood-boosting properties due to its content of theobromine and flavonoids.

Familiarity and Routine: Access to familiar foods like cookies, coffee, or tea can help maintain a sense of routine and normalcy, essential for mental stability during uncertain times. These foods provide a comforting familiarity that can help reduce anxiety and stress.

Shared Experiences: Comfort foods often bring people together. Sharing a favorite snack or preparing a familiar meal can strengthen social bonds and create a sense of community, even under challenging circumstances. For example, preparing pancakes with syrup for breakfast can bring a sense of family unity and normalcy.

Preventing Food Fatigue

The diet might become monotonous in a survival scenario due to limited food choices. Comfort foods add variety and satisfaction to your meals, preventing food fatigue and ensuring that meals remain something to look forward to. Items like granola bars, instant oatmeal, or pudding cups can break the monotony of a repetitive diet.

Nutritional Benefits

While comfort foods are often associated with indulgence, many of them also provide essential nutrients and quick energy, which can be especially beneficial in survival situations:

Quick Energy: Comfort foods like honey, chocolate, and granola bars are rich in carbohydrates, providing a fast and easily accessible energy source. This is particularly important during physical exertion or high stress when the body needs rapid fuel.

Healthy Fats and Protein: Items like peanut butter or nut butters are comforting and provide healthy fats and protein, which help keep you full and sustain energy levels. These are particularly important in maintaining energy when meals might be spaced out, or resources are limited.

Antioxidants: Some comfort foods, like dark chocolate and green tea, are high in antioxidants, which help combat oxidative stress and support overall health. These nutrients are precious during prolonged periods of stress or when fresh fruits and vegetables are scarce.

Portion Control

While comfort foods are essential, managing their consumption is crucial, especially in a survival situation where resources are limited. Opt for portion-controlled packaging to help regulate intake and ensure that these items last as long as needed.

Examples

Chocolate: A quick morale booster, especially dark chocolate, is rich in antioxidants and has mood-enhancing properties.

Cookies: Shelf-stable cookies or biscuit tins offer a sweet treat that can lift spirits and provide a sense of normalcy.

Coffee and Tea: Essential for maintaining daily routines and providing comfort. Coffee is also a natural stimulant, helping to improve focus and energy levels, while tea offers a calming effect.

Hot Cocoa Mix: Instant hot chocolate provides a warm, comforting drink that is incredibly soothing during cold weather or stressful times.

Granola Bars: Portable, energy-dense, and satisfying, granola bars are ideal for quick snacks or breakfast on the go.

Pudding Cups: Pre-packaged pudding offers a creamy, sweet dessert that requires no preparation, making it a convenient comfort food.

Canned Fruit: Items like peaches, pears, or fruit cocktails are refreshing and provide a sweet treat with added nutrients.

Syrup and Pancake Mix: Pancakes with syrup can create a comforting breakfast experience that is both familiar and joyful.

Instant Oatmeal: A warm and satisfying breakfast option that's easy to prepare and provides comfort and nutrients.

Beverages

Beverages are critical in long-term food storage, providing hydration, nutrition, and psychological comfort during emergencies. They help maintain both physical and mental well-being. Below are the key points to consider when stocking essential beverages, organized by their psychological importance, nutritional benefits, preservation qualities, and medicinal uses.

Psychological Importance

Comforting Familiarity: Hot drinks like coffee, tea, or cocoa provide a sense of normalcy and routine, reducing stress.

Mood Boost: Beverages can lift morale during challenging times by adding variety to meals and offering comforting warmth.

Routine Maintenance: Maintaining daily rituals with coffee or tea can provide stability in stressful situations.

Nutritional Benefits

Hydration: Water is vital for life; other beverages help maintain hydration while offering nutritional benefits.

Energy and Focus: Caffeine in coffee and tea can help with mental clarity and physical energy.

Vitamin and Mineral Intake:

- Milk: Provides calcium, protein, and vitamin D.

- Juices: Offer vitamin C and antioxidants, essential for immune support.

- Electrolyte Drinks: Replenish vital minerals like sodium and potassium.

Medicinal Benefits

Herbal Teas: Chamomile, peppermint, and ginger help digestion, nausea, and relaxation.

Electrolyte Drinks: Oral rehydration salts are critical for treating dehydration due to illness or physical exertion.

Honey: Used in beverages like tea. Honey has antibacterial properties and soothes sore throats.

Alcohol (Optional): Spirits can be used for sanitization, bartering, or limited medicinal purposes.

Examples

Shelf-Stable Milk: Powdered milk, evaporated milk, shelf-stable plant-based milk. Provides calcium, protein, and essential vitamins

Instant Coffee and Tea: Instant coffee, tea bags, herbal teas. Energy, focus, and relaxation with herbal options

Electrolyte Drinks: Powdered electrolyte mixes, oral rehydration salts. Replenishes lost electrolytes and helps prevent dehydration.

Juices: Canned fruit juice, powdered juice mixes. Source of vitamin C, antioxidants, and hydration.

Cocoa and Hot Chocolate: Cocoa powder, instant hot chocolate mix. Comfort, warmth, and extra calories.

Alcohol (Optional): Spirits last indefinitely, while wine and beer have shorter storage times. Alcohol is useful for sanitation, bartering, or stress relief in moderation.

Salt & Sugar

Salt and sugar are vital for long-term food storage due to their roles in preservation, flavor enhancement, and caloric provision in the case of sugar. Here's why they are essential

Salt

Preservation: Salt is vital for curing meats, pickling, and preventing bacterial growth. It ensures long-term food safety without refrigeration.

Flavor: Salt enhances the taste of basic foods, making them more palatable.

Nutritional Need: Salt is essential for electrolyte balance and muscle function, especially during physical exertion.

Versatility: Beyond food, salt can be used in fermenting and medical purposes like wound cleaning.

Sugar

Preservation: Sugar is critical for preserving fruits in jams, jellies, and syrups, preventing spoilage by drawing out moisture.

Calories: As a high-calorie food, sugar provides quick energy, making it essential in survival situations.

Flavor and Morale: Sugar sweetens otherwise bland foods and can be used to make treats that boost morale.

Versatility: Useful in baking, fermenting, and even minor medical applications.

Wrapping it Up...

Getting a good grasp on nutrition and diet is vital to creating a sustainable *Food Survival Plan* that keeps you physically and mentally healthy. When you focus on a balanced mix of macronutrients, micronutrients, and essential vitamins, your food storage becomes a way to boost your energy, immunity, and overall well-being, especially during tough times. Mixing in preserved foods, fresh produce when you can, and a variety of flavors from herbs, spices, and condiments keeps things interesting and helps you avoid getting bored with your meals while ensuring your diet stays nutritious and enjoyable.

Key Points

Nutritional Needs: Your diet should contain the right mix of proteins, fats, carbohydrates, vitamins, and minerals to keep your body healthy.
Impact of Preservation Methods: Preserved foods can affect nutrient content. For example, Freezing is good for keeping nutrients, but Canning and Drying can reduce some vitamins.
Superfoods: Adding superfoods like berries, greens, and nuts can boost the nutrition in your diet because they're packed with nutrients.
Caloric Needs: A balanced diet and enough calories will help you stay energized and healthy.
Water: Stay hydrated and get enough water to keep your body running smoothly and maintain your health.
Herbs and Spices: Powerful and versatile ingredients that enhance your meals' flavor, nutritional value, and health benefits.
Condiments and Sauces: Great for improving staple foods' taste, diversity, and nutritional content.
Comfort Foods: Provides a psychological boost, helping to alleviate anxiety and create a sense of familiarity and security.
Beverages: Provides hydration, nutrition, and psychological comfort during emergencies.
Salt & Sugar: Great for flavor and food preservation.

Online Resources

- USDA FoodData Central: Detailed nutritional information for various food items. https://fdc.nal.usda.gov/

- USDA MyPlate: Information on nutrition and healthy eating. Offers a variety of tools, guidelines, and resources to help individuals and families make healthier food choices. https://www.myplate.gov/

- Centers for Disease Control and Prevention (CDC) - The CDC provides resources and guidelines on emergency preparedness, including food safety and public health concerns during disasters. https://emergency.cdc.gov/

- EatByDate: Provides information on food shelf life and tips on managing special dietary needs within a stockpile. https://eatbydate.com/

3

FOOD SOURCES

Rice is a staple for over half the world's population and has been cultivated for at least 9,000 years

A key aspect of long-term food security for preppers is the understanding and diversification of food sources. Depending on just one type of food can be risky during emergencies or survival situations, so it's essential to have a comprehensive plan that includes various accessible food options. To ensure sustainability and nutritional balance, these options include fresh, locally sourced foods and long-lasting, shelf-stable items, including store-bought products. Having a range of food sources allows you to adapt to changing situations, lessen reliance on any food type, and enhance your overall preparedness.

Fresh Food

Fresh food is essential for getting the nutrients missing in preserved or processed options, especially vitamins, minerals, and fiber. While fresh foods do spoil faster, preppers can still work them into their long-term plans with a few handy strategies:

Gardening: Growing your own fruits, vegetables, and herbs ensures a renewable supply of fresh produce. Home gardening provides self-sufficiency and variety, whether in a backyard or in containers. Crops like tomatoes, lettuce, carrots, and potatoes can be grown seasonally. At the same time, herbs like basil and mint are easy to cultivate for flavor and nutrition.

Foraging: Wild edibles, such as berries, nuts, mushrooms, and leafy greens, are valuable fresh food sources. Knowing how to identify and safely harvest wild plants can provide access to food in areas where cultivation isn't possible.

Livestock and Small Animals: Raising chickens for eggs, goats for milk, or rabbits for meat offers a steady, fresh protein supply. Small livestock can be a sustainable food source for preppers with the space and resources that complement stored goods.

Hunting and Fishing: In rural or wilderness areas, hunting game and fishing are reliable ways to obtain fresh meat. Fresh protein from wild animals is a valuable supplement to preserved foods. Still, hunting and fishing require skill, equipment, and adherence to local regulations.

Through DIY food preservation, you can extend the shelf life of fresh foods. In the upcoming chapters, we will explore various DIY food preservation methods in detail.

Canned Foods

Canned goods have become a dietary mainstay for their convenience and longevity. Their airtight seals and thorough cooking eliminate the need for refrigeration, ensuring a long shelf life. This makes them ideal for long-term food security, offering a wide variety of options that can be easily stored.

Benefits

- Versatile, requires minimal preparation, and can last for years when stored properly.
- They provide a good mix of nutrients and can easily be incorporated into meals.

Common Canned Foods

Vegetables and Fruits: Green beans, corn, peas, carrots, peaches, and pineapples provide essential vitamins and minerals.

Proteins: Canned meats like tuna, chicken, beef, and beans offer shelf-stable protein sources that are easy to prepare.

Prepared Meals: Soups, chili, stews, and canned pasta provide convenient, ready-to-eat meals that only need to be heated.

Dry Foods

Dry foods are easy to stash away and last a long time, which is why they're a key component of any prepper's *Food Survival Plan*. They don't take up much room and can be kept in airtight containers to keep them fresh.

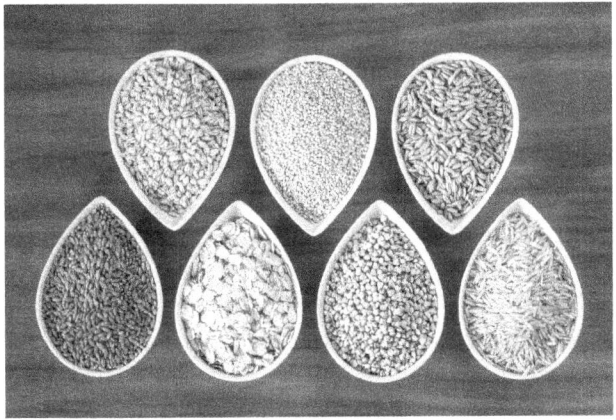

Benefits

- Dry foods are compact, lightweight, and last for a long time when stored in cool, dry environments.

- They are also cost-effective, allowing preppers to buy in bulk and stretch their food budget.

Common Dry Foods

Grains: Rice, quinoa, oats, and pasta are all excellent sources of carbohydrates and fiber. These dry goods can form the basis of meals and have a shelf life of several years.

Legumes: Dried beans, lentils, and peas are rich in protein and fiber, and they store well in bulk. They can be rehydrated and cooked in a variety of ways.

Flours and Baking Ingredients: Flour, cornmeal, powdered milk, and sugar are essential for making bread and other baked goods. They are also versatile ingredients that complement other preserved foods.

Protein Bars and Drinks

Protein bars and drinks are perfect for a quick energy boost and essential nutrients, especially when you need something portable and easy to grab.

Protein Bars

- Designed to be high in protein and calories, making them an ideal choice for survival situations.
- They are compact and have a long shelf life, usually lasting up to two years.

Protein Shakes and Powders

- Shelf-stable protein powders can be mixed with water or milk for a quick meal replacement.
- They are lightweight, portable, and can be stored long-term.

Benefits

- Protein bars and shakes are easy to carry, require no preparation, and provide a concentrated source of calories and nutrients.
- They are handy for bug-out bags or emergency kits.

Meals Ready to Eat (MREs)

MREs are complete meals designed for military personnel but are also highly useful for preppers. These meals are fully cooked, shelf-stable, and packed in airtight packaging, meaning they can be eaten without additional preparation.

Key Features

- Typically include an entrée, side dishes, snacks, desserts, and a drink mix.

- They also often come with a heating element that allows them to be warmed without external heat sources.

Benefits

- MREs are convenient, nutritionally balanced, and have a shelf life of up to five years or more.

- They are perfect for short-term emergencies or limited access to cooking facilities.

Store-Bought Long-Life Foods

Store-bought, long-lasting foods are made to last long, making them convenient for preppers who want easy-to-store, ready-to-eat options. These foods are perfect for stockpiling since they're lightweight, compact, and nutritious.

Benefits

- Store-bought long-life foods are designed to have minimal preparation, excellent shelf life (ranging from 5 to 25 years), and compact packaging, making them ideal for both short-term emergencies and long-term storage.

- These foods are also lightweight and portable, perfect for bug-out bags or mobile survival situations.

Common Store-Bought Long-Life Foods

Freeze-Dried Meals: Freeze-dried foods such as vegetables, meats, and complete meals are incredibly lightweight, making them perfect for long-term storage and bug-out bags. They retain much of their nutritional value and only require water for rehydration.

Powdered Milk: A staple for long-term food storage, powdered milk is shelf-stable and provides essential nutrients like calcium and protein.

Instant Oatmeal and Soups: These meals offer quick preparation and long shelf life, making them convenient for short-term emergencies or stockpiling.

Dried Pasta and Rice Mixes: Pre-packaged mixes like instant rice or pasta dishes provide a quick, calorie-dense meal solution that requires minimal cooking.

Shelf-Stable Cheese and Jerky: Vacuum-sealed cheese or jerky can last long and offer portable protein and fat for balanced nutrition.

DIY Preserved Foods

Food preservation is crucial for preparedness. It's the reliable backup supply of nourishment for emergencies or when you're off the grid. They extend the shelf life of your food, ensuring you have access to essential nutrients even in challenging situations.

Your fresh foods can be used for your own DIY food preservation.

Benefits

- Preserved foods store nutritious, homemade items that retain much of their original nutritional value.
- They also provide variety, helping to avoid palate fatigue in long-term survival situations.

Common Preservation Methods

Canning: Foods like fruits, vegetables, and meats are preserved in jars through heat processing.

Dehydrating: Removing moisture from food prevents bacterial growth, extending shelf life. Dried fruits, vegetables, and jerky are common examples.

Fermenting: Fermentation uses beneficial bacteria to preserve food. Sauerkraut, kimchi, and yogurt are examples.

Freeze-Drying: This method removes moisture by freezing and dehydrating food, resulting in lightweight, long-lasting products.

Wrapping it Up...

Mixing up your food sources is vital for staying prepared and surviving in the long run. By adding a variety of foods to your stockpile, you'll set yourself up with a balanced and sustainable *Food Survival Plan* that can get you through emergencies and times when you need to be self-sufficient. Each type of food brings its own perks, whether keeping nutrients intact or being easy to use. They all help ensure you have the calories, nutrients, and flavors you need, no matter what comes your way.

Key Points

Fresh Food: Great for nutrients but only lasts for a short time.
Canned Foods: Convenient and long-lasting, no need for refrigeration.
Dry Foods: Grains, legumes, and more with a long shelf life.
Protein Bars and Drinks: Portable, easily stored sources of protein.
Meals Ready to Eat (MREs): Easy to store and prepare for the long term.
Store-bought Long-Life Foods: These are made to last long, making them convenient for preppers who want easy-to-store, ready-to-eat options.
DIY Preserved Food: Canned, Dehydrated, and Freeze-Dried items keep well and keep their nutrition.

Online Resources

- USDA FoodData Central: Detailed nutritional information for various food items. https://fdc.nal.usda.gov/

- USDA MyPlate: Information on nutrition and healthy eating. Offers a variety of tools, guidelines, and resources to help individuals and families make healthier food choices. https://www.myplate.gov/

- The Ecological Farming Association: Resources and training on ecological farming practices, including food preservation methods tailored to specific climates. https://eco-farm.org/

- Ready.gov: A U.S. government website that offers comprehensive guides on preparing for emergencies, including food and water storage. http://ready.gov

- EatByDate: Provides information on food shelf life and tips on managing special dietary needs within a stockpile.

4

DIY Food Preservation

In ancient China, people preserved food in clay pots sealed with animal fat for over a year.

We examined your food sources, diet, and nutritional needs in the first few chapters. Now, in this chapter, we will explore different DIY food preservation methods. We'll break it all down with easy-to-follow step-by-step guides, weigh the pros and cons of each method, list the equipment you'll need, and share some troubleshooting tips. Plus, we'll help you choose the right preservation method for your situation.

DIY Preservation vs Store-Bought

When it comes to food preservation, DIY and store-bought, both have their upsides. DIY lets you play with flavors and you know precisely what's in your food; plus, it can be a fun project and save you some cash if you buy in bulk. On the flip side, store-bought options are super convenient, ready to eat, and come in tons of flavors, but they can be pricier and have more packaging waste. The sweet spot? Do some DIY for your favorites, like jams or pickles, and grab store-bought stuff for the things you don't have time to make. That way, you get the best of both worlds.

Here's a table that summarizes the key differences between DIY preservation and store-bought foods:

	DIY Food Preservation	Store-Bought Preserved Foods
Cost Savings	More cost-effective, especially when buying fresh produce in bulk.	Generally more expensive due to processing, packaging, and convenience.
Quality Control	Complete control over ingredients and freshness.	Consistent quality but may include unwanted additives or preservatives.
Customization	Tailor taste and ingredients to personal preferences.	Limited to available varieties and pre-determined flavors.
Nutritional Value	Can retain maximum nutritional value using preferred methods.	Nutrient retention varies; may lose some nutrients during processing.
Sustainability	Reduces packaging waste and promotes reusable containers.	Involves more packaging, contributing to waste.
Convenience	Requires time and effort for preparation and preservation.	Ready-to-eat options, ideal for busy lifestyles and emergencies.
Consistency	Quality may vary depending on technique and experience.	Provides consistent taste and quality.
Shelf Life	Varies by method; typically shorter than commercial options.	Often has a long shelf life due to advanced preservation techniques.
Variety	Limited to what can be preserved at home.	Wide variety of foods, including exotic and hard-to-preserve items.
Accessibility	Requires upfront preparation and equipment.	Readily available in stores, no preparation needed.

DIY Food Preservation

DIY food preservation is a great way to make the most of your food and save money. By learning different methods, you can keep your food fresh and tasty for longer. Whether you're a pro or just starting out, these techniques can help you take charge of your food supply and enjoy delicious homemade treats all year round.

Here are the different ways to preserve food that we'll be looking into:

Water Bath and Pressure Canning: These are the main methods for canning food to last longer.

Dehydration: This technique removes moisture from food to make it last longer, enhance flavors, and keep essential nutrients intact.

Fermentation: This traditional method not only preserves food but also boosts its nutritional value by creating good bacteria.

Freezing: A quick and easy way to keep food fresh whenever needed.

Freeze-Drying: By freezing food and removing moisture through sublimation, this method helps food last longer.

Vacuum Sealing: This modern method keeps food fresh by removing air and preventing oxidation.

Salting / Curing: Preserving food using salt to draw out moisture and create an environment where bacteria can't survive.

Smoking: An old-school way to preserve and add a tasty smoky flavor.

Sugaring: Using high sugar levels to stop microbial growth and extend the shelf life of food.

Pickling: Immersing food in an acidic solution, like vinegar, to prevent spoilage-causing microorganisms from growing.

While it's great to know about all the different food preservation methods we'll cover, most of us will stick to just a few that fit our needs. The goal here is to give you a solid grasp of these methods so you can choose the ones that work best for you.

Choosing the Right Preservation Method

Choosing the right way to preserve your food stockpile is important for keeping it safe and usable over the long haul. Different foods do better with specific preservation methods, so your choice will depend on what kind of food you have, how much space you've got for storage, how long you want it to last, and what tools or time you can dedicate to the process. Each method has its pros and cons, so getting to know them will help you make intelligent decisions and create a flexible, sustainable food supply.

Type of Food

The method you should use depends on the kind of food you're trying to preserve. Some foods work better with certain preservation techniques because of their moisture content, acidity, and texture.

High-Acid Foods (Fruits, Tomatoes, Pickles): These foods are ideal for water bath canning since their acidity helps prevent the growth of harmful bacteria. They can also be dehydrated or freeze-dried if you need lightweight, long-lasting options.

Low-Acid Foods (Vegetables, Meats, Beans): These foods require pressure canning to kill bacteria safely and ensure a long shelf life. Depending on how you store them, you can freeze, freeze-dry, or smoke meats and vegetables.

Leafy Greens and Herbs: Dehydration is the best option for storage for lightweight, long-lasting leafy greens and herbs. You can also freeze-dry them for extended shelf life while retaining their nutritional content.

Fruits: Fruits can be canned, dehydrated, freeze-dried, or preserved through sugaring (such as making jams or candied fruits). The choice depends on whether you prefer a portable dried fruit or a spreadable preserve.

Here's a table listing common foods associated with each DIY preservation method:

	Common Foods
Water Bath Canning (High-acid foods)	Fruits - Apples, Berries, Cherries, Peaches, Pears, Plums, Citrus Fruit Products - Jams, Jellies, Applesauce, Fruit Butter Pickles and Relishes - Cucumber Pickles, Pickled Beets, Relishes
Pressure Canning (Low-acid foods)	Vegetables - Beans, Carrots, Corn, Peas, Potatoes Meats - Beef, Chicken, Pork, Game meats, Chicken, Turkey Seafood - Fish, Crab, Clams, Shrimp Legumes - Beans, Chickpeas, Lentils
Dehydration	Fruits - Apples, Bananas, Berries, Mangoes, Pineapples, Peaches, Pears, Vegetables - Carrots, Tomatoes, Peppers, Onions, Garlic, Zucchini, Spinach Herbs and Spices - Basil, Oregano, Thyme, Rosemary, Parsley, Mint
Fermentation	Fruits - Apples, Grapes, Pineapples Vegetables - Cabbage (Sauerkraut, Kimchi), Cucumbers (Pickles), Beets Dairy - Milk (Yogurt, Kefir), Cream (Sour Cream), Cheese Grains - Wheat (Sourdough Bread), Barley (Beer), Rice (Rice Wine)
Freezing	Fruits - Berries, Apples, Bananas, Peaches, Pineapples, Mangoes, Grapes Vegetables - Carrots, Broccoli, Green Beans, Peas, Corn, Bell peppers Meats - Beef, Chicken, Pork, Fish Dairy - Milk, Cheese, Butter, Yogurt
Freeze Drying	Fruits - Apples, Bananas, Berries, Mangoes, Pineapples, Peaches, Grapes Vegetables - Carrots, Tomatoes, Peppers, Mushrooms, Onions, Garlic, Meats - Beef, Chicken, Turkey, Fish Dairy - Milk, Cheese, Yogurt
Vacuum Sealing	Vegetables - Tomatoes, Peppers, Mushrooms, Onions, Garlic, Spinach Meats - Beef, Chicken, Turkey, Fish Dairy - Milk, Cheese, Yogurt Dry Goods - Coffee Beans, Rice, Pasta Prepared Meals - Soups, Stews, Casseroles, Pasta dishes
Salting/ Curing	Fruits - Plums, Lemons Vegetables - Cabbage (Sauerkraut, Kimchi), Cucumbers (Pickles), Olives Meats - Ham, Bacon, Salami Fish - Salmon, Cod
Sugaring	Fruits - Strawberries, Cherries, Blueberries, Peaches, Plums, Apples, Nuts - Almonds, Pecans, Walnuts Baked Goods - Cookies, Fruitcakes
Smoking	Vegetables - Peppers, Tomatoes, Onions Meats - Beef, Pork, Chicken, Fish, Cheeses - Cheddar, Gouda, Mozzarella Nuts - Almonds, Pecans, Walnut
Pickling	Vegetables - Cucumbers, Carrots, Onions,Beets, Garlic, Green Beans, Peppers, Meats - Fish, Pork, Herring Dairy - Eggs

Available Storage Space

The amount and type of storage space available can influence your choice of preservation method.

Limited Space: If you have limited pantry or storage space, Dehydration and Freeze-drying are great options because they significantly reduce the size and weight of foods. Vacuum Sealing can also help save space by compressing food packages.

Ample Space: Canning is an excellent choice if you can access a large pantry or root cellar. Freezing is another option, but you'll need sufficient freezer space to accommodate bulk storage.

Outdoor or Barn Storage: For those with outdoor storage spaces like barns, smoking and curing meats may be ideal, as they can be stored in cooler, dry areas. Root vegetables like potatoes or carrots can be kept in root cellars without preservation.

Desired Shelf Life

Your preservation method should align with how long you want your food to last.

Short-Term (Up to 1 Year): Freezing and refrigerating fermented foods and water bath canning are suitable for short- to medium-term storage. These methods preserve food quality and nutrition but are generally limited to 6-12 months.

Medium-Term (1-3 Years): Pressure canning and dehydrating extend the shelf life of meats, vegetables, and fruits for up to 2-3 years. These methods maintain food safety for long-term use while taking up relatively little space.

Long-Term (5-25 Years): If your goal is long-term, survival-grade storage, freeze-drying is your best option. Freeze-dried foods can last up to 25 years and are lightweight and easy to store.

Vacuum-sealed dehydrated foods can last several years if stored properly in a cool, dry environment.

Here is a quick look at some common foods and their improved shelf life after food preservation:

	Storage	Shelf Life	Preservation Method	Preservation Shelf Life
Dry Foods				
Rice, Pasta, Beans, Lentils	Cool, dry place, airtight	1-2 years	Vacuum seal	5+ years
Flour, Oats	Cool, dry place, airtight	6-12 months	Vacuum seal	2-3 years
Dried Fruits	Cool, dry place, airtight	6-12 months	Vacuum seal	1-2 years
Powdered Milk	Cool, dry place, airtight	6-12 months	Vacuum seal	2-5 years
Honey, Salt	Cool, dry place, airtight	Indefinite	N/A	Indefinite
Fresh Meat & Poultry				
Chicken	Refrigerator, tightly wrapped	1-2 days	Freeze	9-12 months
Red Meat	Refrigerator, tightly wrapped	3-5 days	Freeze	9-12 months
Fish	Refrigerator, tightly wrapped	1-2 days	Freeze	6-9 months
Baked Goods	Room temperature, airtight	3-5 days	Freeze	2-3 months
Fresh Herbs	Refrigerator	1-2 weeks	Dehydrate	6-12 months
Nuts	Refrigerator, airtight	6 months	Freeze	12 months
Fresh Vegetables				
Carrots	Cool, dark place, unwashed	4-6 months	Blanch and freeze	12-18 months
Potatoes	Cool, dark place, ventilated	2-3 months	Dehydrate	12-18 months
Garlic	Cool, dry, ventilated	3-5 months	Dehydrate	12-18 months
Leafy Greens	Refrigerator, crisper drawer	1-2 weeks	Blanch and freeze	8-12 months
Fresh Fruits				
Apples	Refrigerator, crisper drawer	4-6 weeks	Dehydrate or Freeze	12-18 months
Citrus Fruits	Refrigerator, crisper drawer	3-4 weeks	Can or freeze	12-18 months
Berries	Refrigerator, unwashed	3-7 days	Freeze	12-18 months
Dairy				
Milk	Refrigerator	1 week	Freeze	3-6 months
Cheese	Refrigerator, wrapped	1-4 weeks	Freeze	6-8 months
Yogurt	Refrigerator	1-2 weeks	Freeze	1-2 months

Freeze-Drying is not included in the table but does have a large shelf life of 25 years for most foods.

Other Factors

Nutritional Preservation: Freeze-drying preserves up to 97% of the original goodness. Fermentation is also a win, adding probiotics for gut health. Dehydration, canning, and freezing can zap some vitamins, especially the heat-sensitive ones. However, they still keep enough nutrients to be worthwhile.

Flavor Boost: Smoking and curing preserve and amp up flavors and calories, making them great for protein and fat sources.

Time and Gear: If you're short on time and fancy gadgets, freezing and dehydrating are your best bets. But if you're up for a bit of investment, pressure canning and freeze-drying can pay off in the long run.

Flavor Vibes: Want bold flavors? Try smoking or fermenting. For that fresh taste, freeze-drying is the way to go. And if you have a sweet tooth, making jams or candied fruits is a fun option!

> **Key Takeaway**
>
> Choosing the right preservation method depends on several factors, including the type of food you're preserving, your available space, how long you need the food to last, and your preferences for flavor and nutrition. For preppers, combining these methods ensures a well-rounded and diverse stockpile that can adapt to various needs and scenarios. Whether you're looking to store nutrient-rich superfoods for long-term survival or need quick, space-saving options, understanding the strengths of each preservation method helps you maximize your food supply and maintain variety in your meals for years to come.

Okay, let's look at the different food preservation methods, covering their pros and cons, the equipment you'll need, and easy step-by-step guides.

Water Bath Canning

Canning is a traditional method of preserving food for extended periods. Home canning utilizes glass jars, unlike commercially canned goods that use metal containers. Water Bath Canning is perfect for preserving high-acid foods like fruits, jams, jellies, salsas, pickles, and more. Basically, you fill up jars with the food, dunk them in boiling water for a set time, which removes any bad stuff, and then let them cool to seal in freshness and keep the food safe from spoiling.

Pros

Simplicity: Water bath canning requires minimal equipment, making it accessible for beginners.

Cost-Effective: The equipment needed for water bath canning is generally inexpensive.

Effective for High-Acid Foods (pH 4.6 or lower): This method is perfect for foods with high acidity levels, which naturally inhibit the growth of harmful bacteria like Clostridium botulinum, which causes botulism.

Cons

Limited to High-Acid Foods: This method is unsafe for low-acid foods (e.g., most vegetables, meats, and dairy), which can harbor dangerous bacteria like Clostridium botulinum if not processed at high temperatures.

Risk of Botulism: If not done correctly, there is a risk of botulism—a potentially fatal form of food poisoning. It requires careful adherence to time and acidity guidelines.

Time-Consuming: Preparing and processing jars can be labor-intensive, especially for large batches.

Common Foods Types

High-Acid Foods

Fruits: Apples, berries, cherries, peaches, and plums are ideal candidates due to their natural acidity.

Tomatoes: While typically borderline, lemon juice or citric acid boosts acidity, making them safe for water bath canning.

Jams and Jellies: High sugar content combined with natural fruit acidity makes them perfect for this method.

Pickles: The added vinegar increases acidity, ensuring safety.

Equipment

Large Pot: A deep pot with a lid, large enough to hold jars and allow water to cover them by at least an inch.

Canning Rack: A rack to keep jars off the bottom of the pot and allow water to circulate around them. Cost between $10 to $20 for a standard canning rack.

Jars: Mason jars are specifically designed for canning.

- 4 oz (quarter-pint) jars: A pack of 12 jars is usually priced around $8 to $12.

- 8 oz (half-pint) jars: Typically cost between $10 to $15 for a pack of 12 jars.

- 16-oz (pint) jars: A pack of 12 jars generally costs $12 to $18.

- 32-oz (quart) jars: A pack of 12 jars is often priced between $15 and $20.

- 64 oz (half-gallon) jars: These larger jars can cost around $20 to $25 for a pack of 6 jars

Lids and Bands: Lids that seal properly and bands to secure them during processing.

Jar Lifter: To safely remove hot jars from boiling water. Costs between $5 to $15.

Funnel: For filling jars without spilling.

Bubble Remover: To release air bubbles from the jars before sealing.

Step-By-Step Instructions

1. Prepare Your Equipment: Wash jars, lids, and bands in hot, soapy water. Sterilize jars by boiling them for 10 minutes if processing time is less than 10 minutes. Keep lids in hot water until ready to use.

2. Prepare Your Food: Follow your recipe to prepare the high-acid food you preserve.

3. Fill the Jars: Use a funnel to fill the jars with your pre-

pared food, leaving appropriate headspace (usually 1/4 to 1/2 inch) as specified in your recipe.

4. Remove Air Bubbles: Run a bubble remover or non-metallic spatula around the inside edge of the jar to release trapped air.

5. Wipe the Rims: To ensure a good seal, ensure the jar rims are clean and free from food residue.

6. Apply Lids and Bands: Place the lids on the jars and screw the bands on until fingertip-tight.

7. Process the Jars: Place jars in the canning rack and lower them into the boiling water. Ensure the water covers the jars by at least 1 inch. Cover the pot and boil for the time specified in your recipe.

8. Cool and Seal: After processing, turn off the heat and let the jars sit for 5 minutes. Using the jar lifter, remove the jars and place them on a towel to cool for 12-24 hours. Please do not disturb them during this time.

9. Check the Seal: Check the lids for a proper seal after cooling. The lids should not flex up and down when the center is pressed.

Troubleshooting

Jars Not Sealing Properly:

- Using old or damaged lids.
- Not screwing bands on correctly.
- Not cleaning jar rims properly before sealing.

Liquid Siphoning During Processing:

- Removing jars from the canner too quickly.

Food Spoilage Signs:

- Improper sealing.

- Insufficient processing time.

Pressure Canning

Pressure Canning is a great way to preserve foods with low acidity, such as meats, veggies, and certain fruits. By heating them to around 240 degrees Fahrenheit, you can ensure they're safe from botulism, which can be a worry with low-acid foods. This method helps your food last longer, so you can always have a well-stocked pantry for whatever comes your way.

Pros

Safety: Necessary for low-acid foods that cannot be safely preserved using the water bath method.

Longevity: Extends the shelf life of preserved foods for months or even years.

Nutritional Value: Retains the nutritional content of foods while making them safe for long-term storage.

Cons

Complex Process: This requires more skill and attention to detail than water bath canning, and it has a steeper learning curve for beginners.

Equipment-Intensive: Requires a pressure canner, which can be expensive ($70-$300+) and large, taking up significant storage space.

Risk of Equipment Failure: Improper use of a pressure canner can lead to equipment malfunction or even safety hazards like explosions if not used correctly.

Common Food Types:

Fruits: Apples, peaches, pears, berries, cherries, tomatoes.

Vegetables: Green beans, carrots, beets, potatoes, corn.

Meats: Chicken, beef, pork, fish (pressure canning).

Soups and Stews: Chicken soup, beef stew, chili.

Jams and Jellies: Strawberry jam, grape jelly, marmalade.

Equipment

Pressure Canner: A specialized pot designed to reach the high temperatures needed for pressure canning.

- Small Pressure Canners (up to 10 quarts): Typically range from $70 to $150.

- Medium Pressure Canners (10 to 16 quarts): Usually priced between $100 to $200.

- Large Pressure Canners (over 16 quarts): Can range from $150 to $300 or more.

Jars: Mason jars are specifically designed for canning.

Lids and Bands: Lids that seal properly and bands to secure them during processing.

Jar Lifter: To safely remove hot jars from the canner.

Funnel: For filling jars without spilling.

Bubble Remover: To release air bubbles from the jars before sealing.

Step-By-Step Instructions

1. Prepare the Canner: Place the rack and the required amount of water per the instruction manual.

2. Prepare the Jars: Clean and fill with prepared food, leaving a one-inch headspace. Add boiling water if necessary, remove air bubbles, wipe rims, apply lids, and tighten bands to fingertip tightness.

3. Load the Canner: Place jars on the rack in the canner. Secure the lid and heat on high.

4. Vent the Canner: Once steam pours from the vent pipe, vent for 10 minutes before closing the vent.

5. Process: Bring the canner to the required pressure. Start the timer based on your altitude and the food you are canning. Maintain the pressure for the recommended time.

6. Cool the Canner: Turn off the heat and let the canner depressurize naturally. Once depressurized, open the canner carefully, remove the jars, and let them cool undisturbed for 24 hours before checking the seals.

Troubleshooting

Jars Not Sealing: Check jar rims for chips or cracks. Ensure pressure is maintained during processing.

Loss of Liquid from Jars: Allow pressure to release naturally and slowly. Sudden changes in pressure can cause liquid to spill out of the jar.

Dehydration

Dehydrating food is a classic way to keep it fresh and full of nutrients. It's different from canning because it removes moisture, preventing bacteria and mold from growing. This helps food last longer and keeps nutrients intact better than boiling or freezing. Dehydrated foods are packed with vitamins and minerals and are great for quick energy since they're smaller. They're perfect for emergency supplies or when you're out hiking with a light backpack.

Pros

Extended Shelf Life: Dehydrated foods can last months to years when stored properly.

Nutrient Retention: Dehydration preserves the nutritional value of food.

Lightweight and Compact: Dehydrated foods are easy to store and transport.

Versatility: Suitable for various foods, including fruits, vegetables, meats, and herbs.

Flavor Concentration: Dehydration enhances the natural flavors of food.

Cons

Energy-Intensive: Dehydrating can take several hours to days, depending on the food and method, and can consume a significant amount of electricity if using an electric dehydrator.

Texture Changes: Dehydrated foods can become tough, leathery, or brittle, which might not be suitable for all culinary uses.

Common Food Types

Fruits: Apples, bananas, grapes (raisins), mangoes, berries.

Vegetables: Tomatoes, carrots, bell peppers, zucchini, mushrooms.

Meats: Beef (jerky), chicken, fish.

Herbs and Spices: Basil, oregano, thyme, parsley, garlic.

Grains and Legumes: Rice, lentils, beans, pasta.

Equipment

Dehydrator: A dedicated food dehydrator with adjustable temperature settings.

- Small Dehydrators (basic models, 4-5 trays): Typically range from $30 to $60.
- Medium Dehydrators (6-10 trays, with adjustable temperature settings): Usually priced between $70 to $150.
- Large Dehydrators (10+ trays, with advanced features like digital controls and timers): Can range from $150 to $300 or more

Oven: An alternative to a dehydrator, though it may be less efficient.

Mandoline or Slicer: For uniform slicing of fruits and vegetables.

Blender or Food Processor: This makes fruit leathers or vegetable powders.

Parchment Paper or Silicone Mats: These are used to line trays and prevent sticking.

Airtight Containers: Jars, vacuum-seal bags, or mylar bags for storing dehydrated foods.

Desiccant Packs: To absorb any remaining moisture and prolong shelf life.

- Small Packs: A pack of 50 to 100 desiccant packs typically costs around $5 to $10.

- Medium Packs: Usually priced between $10 to $20 for 50 to 100 packs.

- Large Packs: Often range from $15 to $30 for 10 to 50 packs.

Step-by-Step Instructions

To get started with dehydrating, you'll first want to select the appropriate method and equipment:

Air Drying:

- Suitable for herbs and some produce under very low humidity.

- Requires a dry, ventilated space.

- It can be inconsistent and slower compared to electric dehydration.

Electric Dehydrating:

- More consistent and can handle a variety of foods, including meats.

- Allows you to control the temperature and is generally faster.

- Ideal for fruits, vegetables, and meats.

Steps

1. Prepare the Food: Wash and clean the food thoroughly. Peel, core, and slice fruits and vegetables uniformly. Trim excess fat from meats.

2. Blanching (For Certain Vegetables): Blanch vegetables such as carrots, broccoli, and green beans by boiling them for 1-2 minutes, then immediately transferring them to ice water. This step is optional but helps preserve color and texture.

3. Arrange on Trays: Arrange the food in a single layer on dehydrator trays or oven racks. Avoid overlapping pieces to ensure even drying.

4. Set Dehydrator Temperature:
    - Fruits: 135°F
    - Vegetables: 125°F
    - Herbs: 95°F
    - Meats: 160°F

5. Drying Time: Drying times vary depending on the type of food, thickness of slices, and humidity levels:
    - Fruits: 6-16 hours
    - Vegetables: 4-12 hours
    - Herbs: 2-4 hours
    - Meats: 4-8 hours

6. Check for Doneness: Fruits should be pliable but not sticky or moist. Vegetables should be brittle or leathery. Herbs should crumble easily. Jerky should be dry and

firm.

7. Cool and Condition: Allow dehydrated food to cool completely. For fruits and vegetables, condition by placing them in a loosely packed container for a few days, shaking daily to distribute any remaining moisture evenly.

8. Store: Allow dehydrated food to cool completely. For fruits and vegetables, condition by placing them in a loosely packed container for a few days, shaking daily to distribute any remaining moisture evenly.

Rehydration

Rehydrating dehydrated foods is a simple process that restores their moisture content, preparing them for cooking or eating. The following steps outline the primary method for rehydrating various dehydrated foods.

1. Submerge Food: Add enough water or liquid (such as broth, juice, or milk) to a container to completely cover the food.

2. Soak Time: Allow the food to soak and absorb the liquid. The soaking time varies depending on the type and size of the dehydrated food:

    - Vegetables: Soak for 15-30 minutes.

    - Fruits: Soak for 20-45 minutes.

    - Meats: Soak for 1-2 hours or overnight in the refrigerator.

    - Grains and Legumes: Soak for 2-8 hours or overnight in the refrigerator.

3. Drain Excess Liquid: Drain any excess liquid. You can use

the soaking liquid in your cooking to retain nutrients and flavor.

Following these steps, you can effectively rehydrate dehydrated foods, restoring them to their original texture and flavor and preparing them for your favorite recipes.

Troubleshooting

Uneven Drying:

- Ensure food pieces are sliced uniformly.
- Rotate trays periodically during drying.
- Avoid overloading the dehydrator or oven.

Food Is Not Drying:

- Check the temperature settings and ensure they are appropriate for dehydrated food.
- Increase air circulation by opening vents or using a fan.

Loss of Flavor or Nutrients:

- Blanch vegetables before dehydrating them to preserve color and nutrients.
- Store dehydrated food away from light and heat to prevent degradation.

Mold Growth:

- Ensure food is fully dehydrated before storing.
- Use airtight containers with desiccant packs.
- Check for moisture regularly, and condition dried foods

properly.

Rehydrated Food Is Mushy:

- Use less water when rehydrating.
- Rehydrate foods slowly in the refrigerator for better texture.

Fermentation

Fermentation is an excellent process that changes foods, making them even better for you and adding good probiotics. It's all about using natural bacteria to turn sugars and starches into lactic acid, which makes food last longer and boosts its health benefits. Eating fermented foods like sauerkraut and kimchi can really up your overall health game.

Pros

Enhanced Nutritional Value: Fermentation increases the bioavailability of vitamins and minerals and adds beneficial probiotics.

Improved Digestion: Probiotics and enzymes in fermented foods aid digestion and promote gut health.

Extended Shelf Life: Fermentation preserves food for months to years when stored properly.

Rich Flavors: Fermentation develops complex flavors and textures that enhance culinary experiences.

Cost-Effective: Requires minimal equipment and ingredients.

Cons

Requires Monitoring: Fermentation is a live process that needs to be closely watched. The balance of salt, temperature, and time is crucial, and improper monitoring can lead to spoilage.

Intense Flavors: The tangy, often sour flavors of fermented foods may only appeal to some, limiting their culinary use.

Common Food Types

Vegetables: Cabbage (sauerkraut, kimchi), cucumbers (pickles), carrots, beets.

Dairy Products: Milk (yogurt, kefir), cream (sour cream), cheese.

Beverages: Kombucha, beer, wine, cider.

Soy Products: Soybeans (tempeh, miso, soy sauce).

Equipment / Ingredients

Fermentation Vessels: Glass jars, ceramic crocks, or food-grade plastic containers.

- Small Glass Fermentation Jars (16-32 oz): These typically cost $10 to $20 for a single jar, which is often equipped with an airlock or lid designed for fermentation.

- Medium Glass or Ceramic Fermentation Crocks (1-2 gallons): These are usually priced between $30 and $70 and often include weights and lids.

- Large Ceramic or Stoneware Fermentation Crocks (3-5 gallons): Depending on the brand and craftsmanship, they can cost $70 to $150 or more.

- Stainless Steel Fermentation Vessels (various sizes, often 1-7 gallons) typically cost $100 to $300 or more, depending on size and features like spigots or pressure valves.

Weights: To submerge food in the brine (glass or ceramic weights, clean stones, or smaller jars).

Airlocks: Optional to allow gasses to escape while keeping air out.

Lids or Cloth Covers: To cover the fermentation vessels.

Salt: Non-iodized salt, such as sea salt or pickling salt.

Water: Non-chlorinated water to avoid killing beneficial bacteria.

Clean Utensils: Spoons, tongs, and knives are used to prepare and handle food.

Step-by-Step Instructions

1. Prepare the Vegetables: Wash and shred or chop the vegetables (e.g., cabbage for sauerkraut).

2. Add Salt: Place the vegetables in a large bowl and sprinkle with non-iodized salt (about 1-3 tablespoons per quart of vegetables). The salt draws out water and creates a brine.

3. Massage the Vegetables: Massage the salt into the vegetables until they release enough liquid to create a brine.

4. Pack the Vegetables: Pack the vegetables tightly into a fermentation vessel, pressing down firmly to eliminate air pockets and ensure the vegetables are submerged in the brine.

5. Add Weights: Place a weight on top of the vegetables to keep them in the brine.

6. Cover the Vessel: Cover the fermentation vessel with a lid or cloth to remove dust and pests while allowing gasses to escape. If using an airlock, attach it to the lid.

7. Ferment: Place the vessel in a cool, dark place at a stable temperature between 60-75°F (16-24°C). Fermentation time can vary from a few days to several weeks, depending on the recipe and desired flavor.

8. Check and Taste: Check the ferment daily, ensuring the vegetables remain submerged in the brine. Taste the ferment periodically until it reaches the desired flavor and tanginess.

9. Store: Once fermentation is complete, transfer the ferment to the refrigerator or a cool, dark place to slow the fermentation process. Properly stored, fermented foods can last for several months.

Troubleshooting

Mold Growth:

- Remove any mold on the surface immediately. Ensure vegetables remain fully submerged in the brine.

- Use weights and check for proper salt concentration to prevent mold.

Ferment Is Too Salty:

- Adjust the amount of salt in future batches according to taste.

- Rinse the fermented vegetables lightly before consuming them to reduce saltiness.

Ferment Is Not Tangy Enough:

- Allow more time for fermentation. Some ferments take longer to develop desired flavors.
- Check the temperature and ensure it is within the optimal range for fermentation.

Unpleasant Odors:

- Ensure proper ventilation and temperature control.

Bubbles or Foam:

- Bubbles and foam are normal during fermentation and indicate active microbial activity.
- Ensure the ferment is adequately vented to allow gasses to escape.

Freezing

Sticking food in the freezer is wise to keep it tasting great for longer. When you freeze food, you hit the pause button on any bacteria or enzymes that might mess with its quality. This means you can enjoy that same flavor and texture whenever you're ready to chow down. Plus, freezing food allows you to plan your meals without being limited by what's in season.

Pros

Nutrient Retention: Freezing preserves the nutritional value of food, maintaining vitamins and minerals.

Extended Shelf Life: Extends the shelf life of foods from a few days to several months or even years.

Convenience: Allows for preserving prepared meals and ingredients, reducing food waste and saving time.

Versatility: Suitable for various foods, including raw and cooked items.

Flavor and Texture: Maintains the taste and texture of foods when done correctly.

Cons

Requires Consistent Power: Freezing is dependent on continuous power. Power outages can lead to thawing and potential food spoilage if the outage is prolonged.

Space-Consuming: Freezers can quickly become full, especially with bulk storage, limiting the amount of food you can preserve.

Texture Changes: Some foods, like leafy greens and high-water-content fruits, may become mushy or lose their texture after thawing

Common Food Types

Fruits: Berries, apples, peaches, cherries, mangoes.

Vegetables: Peas, corn, green beans, broccoli, spinach, carrots.

Meats: Beef, chicken, pork, fish, seafood.

Dairy Products: Cheese, butter, milk, yogurt.

Prepared Meals: Soups, casseroles, pasta dishes, stews.

Equipment

Freezer: A standard freezer, deep freezer, or chest freezer, depending on storage needs.

Freezer Bags/Containers: Airtight, freezer-safe bags, containers, or vacuum-seal bags to prevent freezer burn.

*Vacuum Sealer***:** Optional but highly effective in removing air from packaging.

- Basic Vacuum Sealers: Typically range from $30 to $70. These models are usually compact, with manual sealing options, and are suitable for occasional use.

- Mid-Range Vacuum Sealers: These models are usually priced between $70 and $150. They often offer more robust features, such as automatic sealing, multiple settings for different types of food, and stronger suction power.

- High-End Vacuum Sealers: Can range from $150 to $300 or more. They are often commercial-grade machines with advanced features like adjustable vacuum strength, pulse functions for delicate items, and built-in storage for rolls of vacuum sealing bags.

- Chamber Vacuum Sealers: Typically range from $300 to $1,000 or more. These are designed for heavy-duty use and allow vacuum-sealing liquids and wet items without the mess, making them ideal for serious home cooks or commercial kitchens.

Freezer Labels and Markers: These are for labeling and dating stored items.

Baking Sheets: These are for flash-freezing individual items before bagging.

Blanching Equipment: Large pot, ice water, and colander for vegetables.

Step-by-Step Instructions

1. Prepare the Food: Wash and clean the food thoroughly. Cut, chop, or portion as needed for future use.

2. Blanching (For Vegetables): Blanch vegetables by boiling them for 2-3 minutes, then immediately transferring them to ice water to stop cooking. Drain thoroughly.

3. Fruits: Blanching is unnecessary for fruits, but treating them with ascorbic acid (vitamin C) can help preserve color and prevent oxidation. You can do this by dipping them in water and ascorbic acid or using commercial ascorbic acid products designed for preserving fruits.

4. Flash Freezing (Optional): For individual items like fruits, vegetables, or meat pieces, arrange them in a single layer on a baking sheet and freeze until solid. This prevents clumping.

5. Packaging: Place the food in freezer-safe bags or containers. Remove as much air as possible to avoid freezer burn. Vacuum sealers are highly effective for this purpose.

6. Label and Date: Label each package with the contents and the freezing date.

7. Freeze: Place the packaged food in the freezer. Arrange items so that air can circulate freely around them to ensure quick and even freezing.

8. Storage: Organize the freezer to keep older items at the front and newer items at the back to ensure proper rotation and use.

Organizing Your Freezer

Efficient freezer organization is essential to maintaining the quality of your frozen foods. An organized freezer minimizes the time spent searching for items. It reduces the amount of warm air introduced each time it's opened.

Tips for Freezer Organization:

Use Clear Containers: Clear, airtight containers or freezer bags allow you to see the contents easily.

Label Everything: Label each package with the contents and the frozen date. This helps keep track of storage duration.

Categorize: Organize the contents by type—store all vegetables in one area and meats in another, and prepare meals separately.

Use Dividers: If you have a chest freezer, use baskets or dividers to separate different types of food. This aids in organization and ensures older items are used before newer ones.

Thawing

Thawing correctly is essential for preserving their quality and ensuring they eat safely.

Safe Thawing Methods:

- *Refrigerator Thawing:* The safest way to thaw frozen food. This method requires planning, as it takes time.

- *Cold Water Thawing:* Place food in a leak-proof plastic bag and submerge it in cold water, changing it every 30 minutes.

- *Microwave Thawing:* This is the fastest method, but if not managed carefully, it can lead to uneven thawing and cooked edges.

Post-Thawing Tips:

- *Cook Immediately:* Once thawed, especially meat and seafood, cook immediately to prevent bacterial growth.

- *Avoid Refreezing Raw:* Once thawed, raw meat should not be refrozen without cooking first to ensure safety.

Troubleshooting

Freezer Burn:

- Ensure food is adequately packaged with minimal air exposure. Use airtight bags and containers.

- Avoid fluctuating freezer temperatures, which can cause moisture loss and freezer burn.

Loss of Texture:

- Blanch vegetables before freezing to maintain texture.

- Avoid freezing high-water content fruits and vegetables raw, as they can become mushy upon thawing.

Off Flavors:

- Use freezer-safe and airtight packaging to prevent the transfer of odors and flavors.

- Do not store foods with strong odors near delicate items like fruits and dairy.

Excessive Ice Crystals:

- Ensure food is thoroughly dried before packaging.

- Flash freeze individual items before bagging to reduce ice crystal formation.

Slow Freezing:

- Arrange items in a single layer and avoid overloading the freezer to allow for quick freezing.

- Ensure the freezer is set to the correct temperature (0°F or -18°C).

Freeze-Drying

Freeze-drying, also known as lyophilization, is a highly effective method of food preservation. It removes moisture while keeping all the good stuff like nutrients, taste, and texture intact. This process makes food last longer, perfect for storing food for a long time or in emergencies. Freeze-dried foods are light and easy to store and carry around, making them handy for long-term storage and emergencies. Just remember that freeze-drying equipment can be pricey, and freeze-dried foods may cost more than other preserved foods.

Pros

Extended Shelf Life: When properly stored, freeze-dried foods can last up to 25 years.

Nutrient Retention: Retains most of the food's nutrients, flavor, and color.

Lightweight and Portable: Reduced weight makes it easy to transport.

No Refrigeration Needed: Can be stored at room temperature.

Versatility: Suitable for a wide range of foods, including fruits, vegetables, meats, and complete meals

Cons

High Initial Cost: Freeze-drying equipment is expensive, ranging from $2,000 to $5,000 or more, making it less accessible for casual users.

Complex and Time-Consuming: The freeze-drying process is lengthy, takes up to 24 hours or more, and requires specialized equipment.

Texture Changes: While freeze-dried foods can be rehydrated, they may not fully regain their original texture, which might not be ideal for all culinary uses.

Common Food Types

Fruits: Strawberries, bananas, apples, peaches, blueberries.

Vegetables: Peas, corn, green beans, broccoli, carrots.

Meats: Chicken, beef, pork, fish.

Dairy Products: Cheese, milk, yogurt.

Complete Meals: Pasta dishes, stews, scrambled eggs, soups.

NOT Suitable: Foods with high fat, sugar, or moisture content.

Equipment

Freeze-Dryer: A home freeze-dryer, like those made by companies like Harvest Right.

- Small Freeze Dryers: Typically range from $2,000 to $3,000. These are suitable for home use and can handle small batches of food.
- Medium Freeze Dryers: Usually priced between $3,000 and $4,500. These are designed for larger batches and are often used by serious home preservers or small businesses.

Vacuum Pump: Usually included in the freeze-dryer, essential for creating the vacuum environment needed for sublimation.

Trays: For spreading food in thin layers to ensure even freeze-drying.

Mylar Bags or Airtight Containers: For storing freeze-dried food.

Oxygen Absorbers: To prevent oxidation and extend shelf life.

Sealer: For sealing Mylar bags.

Step-by-Step Instructions

1. Prepare the Food:

    - Clean and Cut: Wash and cut the food into uniform pieces to ensure even freeze-drying.
    - Blanching (Optional): Blanching can help preserve

color and texture for some vegetables.

2. Pre-Freeze the Food:

       - Arrange on Trays: Spread the food in a single layer on the freeze-dryer trays.

       - Pre-Freeze: Place the trays in the freezer to pre-freeze the food. This step can speed up the freeze-drying process.

3. Load the Freeze-Dryer:

       - Place Trays: Insert the trays into the freeze-dryer.

       - Close the Door: Ensure the freeze-dryer door is securely closed to create a vacuum seal.

4. Start the Freeze-Drying Process:

       - Set Parameters: Follow the manufacturer's instructions to set the appropriate freeze-drying parameters for your specific food type.

       - Begin Freeze-Drying: Start the freeze-dryer. Depending on the food and machine, the process can take 24 to 48 hours.

5. Check for Doneness:

       - Inspect the Food: Once the cycle is complete, check the food to ensure it is thoroughly freeze-dried. It should be scorched and brittle.

6. Store the Freeze-Dried Food:

       - Packaging: Place the freeze-dried food in Mylar bags or airtight containers.

       - Add Oxygen Absorbers: Include oxygen absorbers in

the packaging to extend shelf life.

- Seal: Use a heat sealer to seal Mylar bags or ensure airtight closure of containers.

Troubleshooting

Incomplete Drying: Increase drying time, check vacuum pressure, and ensure food pieces are not too thick enough.

Ice Build-Up: Regularly defrost the vacuum chamber and check the condenser.

Loss of Vacuum: Check for leaks and ensure all connections are tight.

Uneven Drying: Cut food into uniform sizes and arrange in a single layer.

Overheating: Monitor and adjust temperature settings appropriately.

Food Spoilage: Use fresh food, pre-treat properly, and store in airtight containers.

Color Change: Ensure a steady freeze-drying process to prevent rapid color changes.

Rehydration Issues: Ensure complete drying before storage and use proper rehydration methods.

Vacuum Sealing

Vacuum sealing is a great way to keep food fresh by sucking out the air from the packaging. This helps prevent oxidation and stops aerobic microorganisms from growing, which means your food lasts longer and stays nutritious. Usually, people use single-use plastic bags for this, but that raises some environmental issues. The good news is there are eco-friendly options out there that cut down on plastic use.

Pros

Extended Shelf Life: Vacuum sealing can significantly extend the shelf life of food by reducing oxidation and preventing freezer burn.

Nutrient Retention: Helps retain the nutritional value of food by minimizing exposure to air.

Space Efficiency: Vacuum-sealed plastic packages are compact and can save space in the freezer, refrigerator, or pantry.

Health Considerations: Non-plastic vacuum sealing eliminates potential leaching of chemicals from plastics into food.

Versatility: It is suitable for various foods, including meats, vegetables, fruits, and dry goods.

Cons

Requires Equipment: A vacuum sealer and specialized containers are necessary, which can be an added expense. Basic models are affordable, but higher-end models can be costly.

Not Standalone: Vacuum sealing is often used with other preservation methods, like freezing or dehydration, rather than as a standalone method.

Plastic Waste: Plastic vacuum-sealed bags are single-use, which can create a significant amount of non-recyclable plastic waste over time.

Plastic-Free Alternatives

Traditionally, vacuum sealing has relied on single-use plastic bags, contributing to environmental concerns. However, sustainable alternatives are available that minimize plastic usage:

Reusable Silicone Bags

These bags are durable, flexible, and airtight. They can be vacuum-sealed using compatible devices or manual methods.

- Benefits: They are washable, reusable, and reduce plastic waste.

- Considerations: Ensure compatibility with your vacuum sealing device.

Glass Mason Jars with Vacuum-Sealed Lids

Glass jars equipped with specialized lids that can be vacuum-sealed using a handheld vacuum pump or compatible vacuum sealer attachments.

- Benefits: Glass is non-reactive and reusable, ideal for storing dry goods, liquids, and perishables.

- Considerations: Unsuitable for freezing liquids due to expansion; handle glass carefully to prevent breakage.

Beeswax Wraps

Cotton fabric infused with beeswax, jojoba oil, and tree resin creates a malleable wrap that adheres to itself and containers.

- Benefits: Reusable, compostable, and naturally antibacterial, making them suitable for wrapping cheeses, bread, and produce.

- Considerations: It is not recommended for raw meats or

high-moisture foods; regular maintenance is required to retain effectiveness.

Common Food Types

Meats: Beef, chicken, pork, fish (especially for freezing).

Vegetables: Asparagus, broccoli, carrots, green beans.

Cheeses: Cheddar, mozzarella, Swiss, parmesan.

Dry Goods: Coffee beans, rice, pasta, flour, sugar.

Prepared Meals: Leftovers, marinated meats, sous vide meals.

Equipment Using Plastics

Vacuum Sealer: A countertop machine designed for vacuum sealing food in plastic bags.

- Basic Vacuum Sealers: Typically range from $30 to $70. These models are usually compact, with manual sealing options, and are suitable for occasional use.

- Mid-Range Vacuum Sealers: These models are usually priced between $70 and $150. They often offer more robust features, such as automatic sealing, multiple settings for different types of food, and stronger suction power.

- High-End Vacuum Sealers: These can range from $150 to $300 or more. They are often commercial-grade machines with advanced features like adjustable vacuum strength, pulse functions for delicate items, and built-in storage for rolls of vacuum sealing bags.

Vacuum Sealer Bags/Rolls: Special bags or rolls designed for vacuum sealing, available in various sizes.

Marker and Labels: These are used for labeling and dating the sealed packages.

Plastic-Free Equipment

Handheld Vacuum Sealers: Portable devices designed to remove air from compatible silicone bags or jar attachments. Basic models start around $20, with more advanced options ranging from $50 to $150.

Reusable Silicone Bags: These durable, flexible bags are for freezer storage. A set of various sizes costs approximately $20-$30.

Jar Manual Vacuum Sealer Kits: These kits include a manual hand pump, jar sealers for wide-mouth and regular-mouth mason jars, and accessory hoses. They cost $15 to $20.

Beeswax Wraps: Available in various sizes to accommodate food items and containers. Cotton fabric infused with beeswax provides a breathable, reusable wrap for perishable items. Around $15–$25 for a pack of three assorted sizes.

Step-by-Step Instructions

1. Prepare the Food: Clean, peel, and cut the food into appropriate portions. Blanch vegetables if necessary, and allow them to cool completely..

2. Choose Appropriate Packaging: Select a plastic or silicone bag, glass jar, or beeswax wrap suitable for the food type.

3. Seal the Packaging:

- Silicone & Plastic Bags: Place food inside, remove air using a handheld vacuum sealer if available, and seal the bag.

- Glass Jars: Fill the jar, leaving appropriate headspace, place the vacuum-sealable lid on top, and use the vacuum sealer to remove air.

- Beeswax Wraps: Wrap the food, using the warmth of your hands to mold the wrap securely around the item.

4. Label and Date: Use a non-toxic marker to label the sealed bags with the contents and the date of sealing. This helps track freshness and rotate stock.

5. Store Appropriately: Place sealed items in the refrigerator, pantry, or freezer as suitable for the food type.

Troubleshooting

Seal Failure:

- Ensure sealing surfaces are clean and dry.
- Verify compatibility between the vacuum sealer and the chosen packaging.

Food Spoilage:

- Confirm that all air was adequately removed during sealing.
- Store sealed foods at appropriate temperatures.

Difficulty Sealing:

- For jars, check that lids and attachments are properly aligned and functioning.
- With beeswax wraps, ensure they are pliable; refresh them by warming them if necessary.

Salting / Curing

Preserving food through salting and curing has been around for ages. It's all about sucking out the moisture to keep those pesky bacteria and mold at bay. Plus, it gives food a tasty kick and helps it last longer without needing a fridge. Perfect for folks who like to be prepared or live in spots where fresh food is hard to come by.

Pros

Extended Shelf Life: Preserves food for long periods without refrigeration.

Enhanced Flavor: Creates unique, rich flavors often sought in cured meats and fish.

Nutrient Preservation: Helps retain the nutritional value of food.

Versatility: Suitable for various foods, including meats, fish, and some vegetables.

Cost-Effective: Requires minimal equipment and ingredients, making it an affordable preservation method.

Cons

High Sodium Content: The process involves significant amounts of salt, which may not be suitable for individuals on low-sodium diets or those with certain health conditions.

Requires Precision: Curing requires careful control of salt levels, temperature, and time to avoid spoilage or uneven preservation, which can be challenging for beginners.

Texture Changes: Cured foods often become very firm or dry, which may not be desirable for all dishes.

Common Food Types

Meats: Ham, bacon, salami, corned beef, sausages.

Fish: Salmon, cod, herring, sardines.

Vegetables: Cabbage (sauerkraut), cucumbers (pickles).

Fruits: Sometimes used for fruits like plums (umeboshi).

Equipment and Ingredients

Salt: Non-iodized salt (such as kosher or sea salt) is preferred as it does not contain additives that can affect the curing process.

Curing Salts: These include sodium nitrate and sodium nitrite, which are used in small amounts to prevent the growth of bacteria, such as Clostridium botulinum.

Sugar: Often used with salt to balance flavors and aid in preservation.

Spices and Herbs: Used to enhance flavor.

Containers: Non-reactive containers such as glass, plastic, or stainless steel hold food while it cures.

Hooks or Racks: For hanging meats during the curing process.

Weights: To ensure even curing by pressing down on the food.

Thermometer: To monitor the temperature during the curing process.

Gloves: To handle the curing of salts and meat safely.

Step-by-Step Instructions

Dry Curing Method

1. Prepare the Meat: Trim any excess fat and ensure the meat is clean and dry.

2. Mix the Cure: Combine non-iodized salt, curing salts (if using), sugar, and any desired spices and herbs in a bowl.

3. Apply the Cure: Rub the cure mixture evenly over the entire surface of the meat. Make sure all areas are thoroughly coated.

4. Pack the Meat: Place the meat in a non-reactive container. If layering multiple pieces, ensure each piece is fully coated with the cure mixture. Add additional weight on top to ensure even curing.

5. Refrigerate: Cover the container and place it in the refrigerator. The curing time will vary depending on the size and type of meat, typically ranging from a few days to several weeks.

6. Check and Turn: Check the meat daily. Drain any liquid that accumulates and turn the meat to ensure even curing.

7. Rinse and Dry: Once the curing period is complete, rinse the meat thoroughly to remove excess salt. Pat it dry with paper towels.

8. Hang and Dry (Optional): For some meats, such as prosciutto or dry-cured sausages, hanging and air-drying may be necessary. Hang the meat in a cool, dry place with good air circulation.

Wet Curing (Brining) Method

1. Prepare the Brine: Dissolve non-iodized salt, curing salts (if using), sugar, and any desired spices and herbs in water to create a brine solution.

2. Submerge the Meat: Place the meat in a non-reactive container and fully submerge it in the brine. Use a plate or weight to keep the meat submerged.

3. Refrigerate: Cover the container and refrigerate. The brining time will vary depending on the size and type of meat, typically ranging from a few days to several weeks.

4. Check and Turn: Check the meat daily and stir the brine to ensure even curing.

5. Rinse and Dry: Once the brining period is complete, remove the meat from the brine, rinse thoroughly, and pat dry.

6. Cook or Smoke (Optional): The meat may be cooked or smoked after curing, depending on the recipe.

Troubleshooting

Food Is Too Salty:

- Rinse excess salt off the food after curing.

- Adjust the salt quantity in the recipe for the next batch.

Uneven Curing:

- Ensure the salt or cure mix is applied evenly to all food surfaces.
- Turn and massage the food regularly during the curing process.

Spoilage or Mold Growth:

- Maintain proper temperature and humidity levels during curing.
- Use the correct ratio of curing salts and follow the recipe instructions precisely.
- Store cured food in a well-ventilated, cool area.

Sugaring

Preserving food with sugar, or sugaring, is a traditional way to make fruits and veggies last longer. You can stop microorganisms from growing and spoiling your food using sugar in different forms like syrups, jams, and jellies. Sugaring removes moisture and creates an unfriendly environment for bacteria and other germs. The high sugar content stops spoilage-causing bacteria, yeasts, and molds from ruining your food. It's a popular method for preserving fruits because it keeps them fresh and enhances their taste and texture, making them a yummy treat that lasts a long time.

Pros

Extended Shelf Life: Sugar preserves fruits for long periods without refrigeration.

Enhanced Flavor: The natural sweetness of sugar enhances the flavor of preserved fruits.

Versatility: Suitable for a wide variety of fruits and some vegetables.

Nutrient Retention: Preserves the nutritional value of fruits while enhancing their taste.

Ease of Preparation: A simple process with minimal equipment is required.

Cons

High Sugar Content: Sugaring adds a large amount of sugar, which may not be suitable for people with diabetes, those on low-sugar diets, or those concerned about calorie intake.

Limited Application: Sugaring is mainly used for preserving fruits and certain vegetables, limiting its versatility.

Crystallization Risk: Over time, sugars can crystallize, affecting the texture and usability of the preserved food. Proper sealing and storage are essential to prevent this.

Common Food Types

Fruits: Berries, peaches, plums, apples (for jams, jellies, preserves).

Candied Fruits: Orange peel, cherries, ginger.

Baked Goods: Cookies, cakes, fruitcakes (to extend shelf life).

Equipment / Ingredients

Sugar: Granulated sugar, brown sugar, or powdered sugar, depending on the recipe.

Pectin: Natural thickening agent used in making jams and jellies.

Acid: Lemon juice or citric acid to help set the pectin and balance the sweetness.

Cooking Pot: Large, heavy-bottomed pot for cooking the fruit and sugar.

Canning Jars: Sterilized jars are used to store the preserved fruits.

Jar Lifter: This is for safely handling hot jars.

Lid Sealer: For sealing jars to ensure they are airtight.

Funnel: For transferring the hot mixture into jars without spilling.

Thermometer: To monitor the temperature of the mix.

Step-by-Step Instructions

Making Jam or Jelly:

1. Prepare the Fruit: Wash, peel, and cut the fruit into small pieces. For jelly, extract the juice from the fruit.

2. Cook the Fruit: Place the fruit or juice in a large, heavy-bottomed pot. Add sugar and lemon juice or citric acid according to the recipe.

3. Add Pectin: If using pectin, add it to the fruit mixture and stir well. Follow the instructions on the pectin package for the correct amount.

4. Boil the Mixture: Bring the mixture to a rolling boil, stirring constantly to prevent sticking and burning. Use a thermometer to monitor the temperature.

5. Test for Setting: Place a small amount on a chilled plate to test if the jam or jelly is set. If it wrinkles when pushed with a finger, it is ready. If not, continue boiling and test again after a few minutes.

6. Fill the Jars: Using a funnel, carefully ladle the hot mixture into sterilized jars, leaving about 1/4 inch of headspace at the top.

7. Seal the Jars: Wipe the rims of the jars with a clean, damp cloth. Place the lids on the jars and seal them tightly with the lid sealer.

8. Process the Jars: Place the filled jars in a boiling water bath canner, submerging them fully. Process for 5-10 minutes, depending on the recipe.

9. Cool and Store: Remove the jars from the water bath and let them cool on a towel. Once cool, check the seals and

store them in a cool, dark place.

Making Candied Fruit:

1. Prepare the Fruit: Wash and peel the fruit. Cut into thin slices or small pieces.

2. Make the Syrup: Combine equal parts sugar and water in a large pot. Heat until the sugar is completely dissolved, creating a simple syrup.

3. Cook the Fruit: Add the fruit pieces to the syrup and simmer over low heat until the fruit becomes translucent and tender.

4. Dry the Fruit: Remove the fruit from the syrup using a slotted spoon and place it on a wire rack or parchment paper to dry. Allow to dry for several hours or overnight.

5. Coat with Sugar: Once the fruit is dry but still slightly tacky, roll the pieces in granulated sugar to coat.

6. Store: Place the candied fruit in an airtight container and store it in a cool, dry place.

Troubleshooting

Jam or Jelly Did Not Set:

- Ensure proper cooking time and temperature are set per the recipe.
- Use the correct amount of pectin and acid to achieve the desired set.
- Test for doneness using the plate test or a candy thermometer.

Crystallization of Sugar:

- Stir sugar thoroughly until completely dissolved.
- Add a small amount of corn syrup or lemon juice to prevent crystallization.

Mold Growth:

- Ensure jars and lids are sterilized before use.
- Process jars in a boiling water bath to ensure a proper seal.

Smoking

Smoking food is an old-school way to keep it fresh and add a tasty, smoky flavor. It's great for meats and fish, making them last longer and taste better. Exposing food to smoke from burning wood can also stop bacteria from growing and prevent food from spoiling.

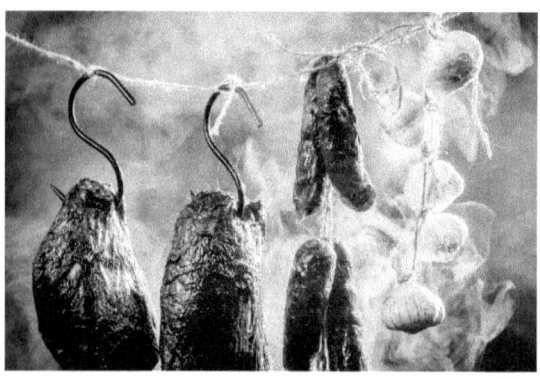

Pros

Extended Shelf Life: Smoking helps preserve food by reducing moisture and inhibiting bacterial growth.

Enhanced Flavor: The smoky flavor adds depth and complexity to the food.

Versatility: Suitable for various foods, including meats, fish, cheeses, and even vegetables.

Nutrient Preservation: Smoking retains the nutritional value of food while adding unique flavors.

Cons

Time-Consuming: Smoking can take anywhere from several hours to several days, depending on the method and the thickness of the food.

Requires Equipment: A smoker or smoking setup is needed, which can range from simple to sophisticated, depending on the method used.

Health Concerns: Regular consumption of smoked foods has been linked to an increased risk of certain cancers due to the presence of carcinogens in smoked products.

Common Food Types

Meats: Beef (brisket), pork (bacon, ribs), chicken, turkey.

Fish: Salmon, trout, mackerel, haddock.

Cheeses: Cheddar, gouda, mozzarella.

Vegetables: Peppers, tomatoes, garlic (for flavoring).

Equipment

Smoker: This can be a dedicated smoker, a grill with a smoking attachment, or a makeshift smoker.

- Portable Smokers: These typically range from $50 to $150. They are small, compact smokers, often electric or charcoal, suitable for casual use and small batches of food.

- Electric Smokers: These smokers are usually priced between $150 and $500. They are user-friendly, with digital controls and consistent temperature maintenance, making them great for beginners and those who prefer a more hands-off approach.

- Charcoal Smokers: Typically range from $100 to $400. These are popular among traditionalists who enjoy managing the fire and smoke themselves. Prices vary based on the size and build quality.

- Propane Smokers: Usually priced between $200 to $500. These offer convenience similar to electric smokers but with the added flavor control from using propane.

- Pellet Smokers: Typically range from $300 to $1,000 or more. These are versatile and can function as both smokers and grills, with digital controls and automated feeding of wood pellets for consistent smoke and temperature.

- Offset Smokers: These large, traditional-style smokers, often used by barbecue enthusiasts for large quantities of food, are usually priced between $200 and $1,500 or more. The price depends on the size, material, and build quality.

- Kamado Smokers (Ceramic, such as the Big Green Egg): These high-end smokers, known for their excellent heat retention and versatility, can range from $300 to $2,000 or more. They are often used for smoking, grilling, and baking.

Wood Chips: Different types of wood (e.g., hickory, apple, cherry) impart different flavors to the food.

Thermometer: To monitor the internal temperature of the smoker and the food.

Water Pan: To maintain moisture in the smoker and prevent the food from drying out too quickly.

Hooks or Racks: For hanging or laying the food inside the smoker.

Fuel Source: Depending on the type of smoker, this could be charcoal, propane, or electricity.

Step-by-Step Instructions

Hot Smoking Method

1. Prepare the Food: Clean and dry the food thoroughly. For meats, consider using a dry rub or marinade to enhance flavor.

2. Preheat the Smoker: Preheat the smoker to the desired temperature (225-250°F). If using a water pan, add water.

3. Add Wood Chips: Soak wood chips in water for at least 30 minutes. Add the soaked wood chips to the smoker box or directly on the coals.

4. Place the food in the Smoker: Arrange it on racks or hang it in the smoker, ensuring enough space for smoke to circulate.

5. Monitor the Temperature: Use a thermometer to keep track of the smoker's internal temperature and adjust vents as necessary to maintain consistent heat.

6. Smoke the Food: Smoke the food for the recommended

time, which varies depending on the type and size. Common smoking times:

- Fish: 1-3 hours

- Poultry: 3-5 hours

- Red meat (e.g., brisket, ribs): 6-12 hours

7. Check Internal Temperature: Use a food thermometer to ensure the internal temperature of the food reaches safe levels (e.g.,165°F for poultry, 145°F for fish).

8. Rest and Store: Allow the smoked food to rest for a few minutes before serving or storing. Store in an airtight container in the refrigerator or freezer.

Cold Smoking Method (for Flavoring Only)

1. Prepare the Food: Clean and dry the food thoroughly. For cheeses and nuts, make sure they are dry to absorb smoke flavor better.

2. Preheat the Smoker: Preheat the smoker to a low temperature (below 90°F) to prevent the food from cooking.

3. Add Wood Chips: Soak wood chips in water for at least 30 minutes. Add the soaked wood chips to the smoker box or directly on the coals.

4. Place the food in the Smoker: Arrange it on racks or hang it in the smoker, ensuring enough space for smoke to circulate.

5. Monitor the Temperature: Use a thermometer to monitor the smoker's internal temperature and adjust vents to maintain a low heat.

6. Smoke the Food: Smoke the food for the recommended

time, which varies depending on the type and size. Typical cold smoking times:

- Cheese: 2-4 hours
- Nuts: 1-3 hours
- Vegetables: 2-6 hours

7. Rest and Store: Allow the smoked food to rest before serving or storing. Store in an airtight container in the refrigerator.

Troubleshooting

Food Is Overly Smoky or Bitter:

- Use the right type and amount of wood chips for your food and smoker.
- Avoid over-smoking; adhere to recommended smoking times.
- Keep the smoker's temperature consistent and within the optimal range.

Uneven Smoking:

- Arrange food in the smoker to allow for even smoke circulation.
- Rotate or reposition the food midway through the smoking process.

Dry or Tough Texture:

- Monitor and maintain proper humidity levels in the smoker.
- Use a water pan if necessary to add moisture to the

smoking environment.

- Avoid overcooking by checking internal temperatures regularly.

Pickling

Pickling is an old-school way to keep your food fresh and tasty. By soaking it in a mix of vinegar, salt, sugar, and spices, you can make your favorite foods last longer and taste even better. The acidic environment created during pickling stops yucky bacteria from growing, so your food stays safe to eat. Plus, pickling works for all kinds of foods, like veggies, fruits, eggs, and meats, giving them a zesty kick that many people love.

Pros

Extended Shelf Life: Pickling extends the shelf life of various foods, allowing for long-term storage.

Enhanced Flavor: The pickling process imparts a tangy, savory flavor to foods, improving their taste.

Nutrient Preservation: Pickled foods retain most nutrients, making them a healthy addition to the diet.

Versatility: Suitable for various foods, including vegetables, fruits, eggs, and meats.

Ease of Preparation: The pickling process is relatively simple and requires minimal equipment.

Cons

High Sodium Content: Pickling typically requires a significant amount of salt, which can be an issue for those on low-sodium diets.

Limited Shelf Life Compared to Other Methods: While pickled foods last longer than fresh produce, their shelf life is shorter than other methods like canning or freeze-drying.

Strong Flavor Profile: The acidic, tangy taste of pickled foods may not appeal to everyone, limiting their use in some dishes.

Common Foods Used

Fish: Herring, shrimp

Vegetables: Cabbage, beets, onions, peppers

Fruits: Apples, mangoes, cherries, peaches

Equipment / Ingredients

Vinegar: Typically white vinegar, apple cider vinegar, or rice vinegar, depending on the recipe.

Salt: Non-iodized salt, such as kosher or pickling salt, does not contain additives that can affect the pickling process.

Sugar: Granulated sugar, brown sugar, or other sweeteners as specified in the recipe.

Spices and Herbs: Dill, mustard seeds, garlic, peppercorns, bay leaves, and other spices to enhance flavor.

Water: Often used to dilute the vinegar solution.

Canning Jars: Sterilized jars with lids for storing the pickled products.

Large Pot: For heating the vinegar solution and processing jars if canning.

Jar Lifter: This is for safely handling hot jars.

Funnel: For transferring the hot brine into jars without spilling.

Lid Sealer: For sealing jars to ensure they are airtight.

Step-by-Step Instructions

Basic Pickling Process

1. Prepare the Vegetables: Wash, peel, and cut the vegetables as desired. Firm vegetables like cucumbers, carrots, and green beans are ideal for pickling.

2. Prepare the Brine: In a large pot, combine vinegar, water, salt, sugar, and spices. A standard ratio is 1 cup of vinegar to 1 cup of water, 1 tablespoon of salt, and 1 tablespoon of sugar. However, this can vary based on the recipe. Bring the mixture to a boil, stirring until the salt and sugar fully dissolve.

3. Pack the Jars: Pack the prepared vegetables tightly into sterilized jars, leaving about 1/2 inch of headspace at the top. If desired, add any additional spices or herbs directly to the jars.

4. Add the Brine: Carefully pour the hot brine over the vegetables in the jars, covering them entirely while maintaining the headspace. Use a funnel to avoid spills.

5. Seal the Jars: Wipe the rims of the jars with a clean, damp cloth to remove any residue. Place the lids on the jars and screw on the bands until fingertip tight.

6. Process the Jars (Optional): If you are canning the pickles for long-term storage, place them in a boiling water bath canner. Ensure the jars are fully submerged in water. Process for 10-15 minutes, adjusting for altitude if necessary.

7. Cool and Store: Remove the jars from the water bath and let them cool on a towel. Once cool, check the seals by pressing down on the center of each lid. If it does not pop back, the jar is sealed. Store sealed jars in a cool, dark place. Unsealed jars should be refrigerated and consumed within a few weeks.

8. Wait Before Eating: For the best flavor, let the pickles sit for at least a week before eating. This allows the flavors to develop fully.

Quick Pickling (Refrigerator Pickling) Method

1. Prepare the Vegetables: Wash, peel, and cut the vegetables as desired.

2. Prepare the Brine: In a pot, combine vinegar, water, salt, sugar, and spices. Bring the mixture to a boil, stirring until the salt and sugar dissolve.

3. Pack the Jars: Pack the vegetables into sterilized jars, leaving headspace.

4. Add the Brine: Pour the hot brine over the vegetables, submerging them fully.

5. Seal and Store: Seal the jars with lids and let them cool to room temperature. Store the jars in the refrigerator. Quick pickles are ready to eat within a few hours but taste best after a few days.

Troubleshooting

Cloudy Brine:

- Ensure the use of non-iodized salt and distilled water.

- Avoid using overripe vegetables, and remove any air

bubbles before sealing.

Pickles Are Too Soft:

- Use fresh, firm vegetables and process them promptly.
- Add calcium chloride (pickle crisp) to maintain crispness.
- Avoid over-processing during the water bath canning stage.

Insufficient Flavor:

- Allow pickles to sit for at least a week to develop flavors fully.
- Adjust spice levels in the brine to match personal taste preferences.

Mold Growth or Spoilage:

- Ensure all jars, lids, and equipment are thoroughly sterilized.
- Check that the jars are sealed properly and stored in a cool, dark place.
- Use the correct ratio of vinegar to water to ensure proper acidity.

Food Preservation Summary Table

Here is a quick reference table of the pros and cons of different food preservation methods:

	Pros	Cons
Water Bath Canning	Simple process Inexpensive equipment	Only high-acid foods Longer processing time Risk of spoilage if not done properly
Pressure Canning	Safe for low-acid foods Kills bacteria and spores Longer shelf life	Needs special equipment Risk of botulism if not done properly
Dehydration	Lightweight and portable Long shelf life Concentrates flavors	Can alter texture Some nutrient loss Time-consuming
Fermentation	Enhances nutritional value Good for gut health Unique flavors	Requires monitoring Limited types of foods Comparable shorter shelf life
Freezing	Preserves nutritional value Convenient Simple process	Requires continuous electricity Limited by freezer space
Freeze Drying	Long shelf life Lightweight & Portable No refrigeration	Equipment is expensive Energy-intensive process Time consuming
Vacuum Sealing	Reduces freezer burn Preserves texture and flavor	Requires special equipment Not suitable for all foods
Salting / Curing	Extends shelf life Enhances flavor	High in sodium Can alter texture Requires time
Sugaring	Long shelf life Preserves color and flavor Simple process	High in sugar Can alter texture Limited types of foods
Smoking	Adds unique flavor Extends shelf life Can combine with other methods	Requires equipment Often time-consuming Health concerns with prolonged consumption
Pickling	Adds unique flavors Long shelf life Preserves texture	High in sodium Some nutrient loss Requires vinegar or brine

Spoilage, Safety, and Shelf Life

When you're getting into DIY food preservation, it's important to know about spoilage risks, safety tips, and how long different methods can keep your food good. Each preservation method has unique factors to consider when preventing spoilage, handling food safely, and making sure your preserved goodies last as long as possible.

Check out this table that breaks down the spoilage, safety, and shelf life info for each preservation method:

	Spoilage Indicators	Safety Tips	Shelf Life
Water Bath & Pressure Canning	Bulging lids, leaking jars, foul odors, discoloration	Use pressure canning for low-acid foods. Ensure jars have a proper seal	12-18 months
Dehydration	Moisture exposure, mold growth, soft or sticky texture, off odors	Ensure foods are fully dried Store in airtight containers	6 months to several years
Fermentation	Foul odors, slimy texture, black or green mold	Maintain a consistent temperature (60-75°F) Use proper salt ratios	6-12 months (refrigerated)
Freezing	Freezer burn, ice crystals, discoloration	Package foods in airtight containers Keep freezer at 0°F (-18°C)	6-12 months
Freeze-Drying	Soft or spongy texture, mold growth	Store in airtight containers (Mylar bags with oxygen absorbers) Keep in a cool, dark place	Up to 20-25 years
Vacuum Sealing	Broken seal, air or moisture exposure	Ensure a tight vacuum seal Inspect bags for punctures	1-3 years (longer if frozen)
Salting / Curing	Slimy texture, discoloration, rancid smell	Use appropriate salt concentration Store in cool, dry conditions	Several months to a year
Sugaring	Mold growth, off smell, fermentation	Store in airtight containers Properly seal jams and jellies	1-2 years
Smoking	Mold growth, unusual smells, slimy texture	Cure meats before smoking Store in cool, dry place or freeze	2-6 months (longer if frozen)
Pickling	Foul odors, discoloration, mold in brine	Ensure brine pH is below 4.6 Store in cool, dark place and refrigerate once opened	6 months to 1 year

Advice for Beginners

Getting into DIY food preservation is a fun and fulfilling experience. It guarantees you'll have a stash of healthy, homemade goodies and save you a good chunk of change in the long run. If you're starting out, the best approach is to keep it simple. Pick a few methods that appeal to you, and then, as you get the hang of things, you can gradually expand your preservation skills.

More Tips

Start with Simple Methods: Begin with straightforward techniques like freezing, dehydrating, or basic canning. These methods require minimal equipment and are easier to master, allowing you to build your skills gradually.

Invest Wisely: Focus on essential, versatile equipment like a good-quality dehydrator, canning jars, or a vacuum sealer. These initial investments may seem costly, but they pay off by extending the shelf life of your food and reducing waste.

Preserve Seasonal Produce: Take advantage of seasonal abundance when fruits and vegetables are at their peak and most affordable. Preserving seasonal produce can save money and provide access to your favorite foods year-round.

Batch Process: Preserve food in batches to save time and energy. Whether you're canning a large quantity of tomatoes or dehydrating a bulk purchase of apples, batch processing is efficient and cost-effective.

Learn from Others: Tap into the knowledge from experienced preservers through online communities or local workshops. Learning from others can help you avoid common pitfalls and improve your techniques.

Keep Track of Costs: Compare your expenses to store-bought preserved foods' costs. Your efforts will likely lead to substantial savings, especially as you refine your processes and reduce waste.

Stay Organized: Proper labeling and storage are crucial for managing your preserved foods. Keeping track of what you have and its expiration date will help you use it efficiently and avoid spoilage.

Ultimately, the time and money you put in at the start can pay off, giving you a pantry stocked with healthy, home-preserved goodies to enjoy all year. With some patience and practice, you'll see that DIY food preservation is a handy skill that saves you cash and boosts your self-sufficiency and food security.

Seasonal Preservation Planning

It's important to plan when preserving food. Don't procrastinate when locking in the goodness of seasonal produce. Setting up a schedule for your preservation tasks throughout the year allows you to enjoy a mix of preserved foods while taking advantage of what each season offers.

Here is a table for crops in season:

	Crops in Season	Preservation Methods	Meal Ideas
January	Potatoes, Winter Squash	Store in cold, dry place	Squash soup, roasted potatoes
February	Carrots, Beets	Pickling, Root cellar storage	Pickled beets, carrot cake
March	Spinach, Kale	Blanch and Freeze	Green smoothies, sautéed greens
April	Asparagus, Radishes	Pickling, Canning	Pickled radishes, asparagus stir-fry
May	Strawberries, Peas	Jams, Freezing	Strawberry jam, pea salad
June	Cherries, Zucchini	Canning, Dehydrating	Cherry preserves, zucchini chips
July	Blueberries, Tomatoes	Jams, Canning	Blueberry muffins, canned tomatoes
August	Peaches, Cucumbers	Canning, Pickling	Peach preserves, pickles
September	Apples, Pears	Drying	Applesauce, dried pears
October	Pumpkins, Sweet Potatoes	Pureeing, Storing	Pumpkin puree, baked sweet potatoes
November	Brussels Sprouts, Cranberries	Freezing, Canning	Cranberry sauce, roasted sprouts
December	Cabbage, Turnips	Fermenting, Storing	Sauerkraut, mashed turnips

Climate Challenges

Food preservation is vital for ensuring a stable food supply. Still, the effectiveness of various preservation methods really hinges on the local climate, which can present its own challenges.

Tropical and Humid Climates

Drying foods in humid areas can be tricky. It might affect your preserved goodies' safety, quality, and shelf life. Here are some of the main challenges you might face and some tips to tackle them when drying foods in humid climates:

Challenges

Inconsistent Drying: High humidity leads to uneven drying and mold growth. Extended drying times increase spoilage risks.

Mold and Bacterial Growth: Foods reabsorb moisture after drying, leading to contamination unless appropriately stored.

Energy-Intensive Solutions: Dehydrators are necessary but costly and energy-intensive.

Limited Sun-Drying: Frequent rain and pests complicate sun-drying, reducing effectiveness.

Storage Challenges: High humidity shortens the shelf life of dried foods, requiring careful storage.

Pest Infestations: Warm, humid conditions attract pests that can contaminate stored foods, making pest control costly and complex.

Strategies

Solar Dryers: Used for consistent drying and reducing spoilage.

Desiccants in Storage: Incorporate desiccants to absorb moisture and protect dried foods.

Vacuum Sealing: Vacuum-seal dried foods to prevent moisture absorption and pest infestation.

Improve Air Circulation: Enhance air circulation during drying to reduce moisture and prevent mold.

Low-Cost Dehumidification: Implement affordable dehumidification methods to complement drying.

Integrated Pest Management: Use natural pest control strategies to reduce contamination risks.

Community Solutions: Invest in shared drying facilities to make advanced methods accessible.

Monitor Fermentation: Regularly monitor fermentation processes to prevent over-fermentation.

To keep food fresh in humid climates, you may need to tweak your preservation methods and look into options like solar dryers, desiccants, and better storage solutions. By using these strategies, you can ensure food security even when the weather presents challenges.

Arid and Desert Climates

Desert and arid climates come with their own set of challenges when it comes to keeping food fresh. The intense heat, lack of water, and low humidity can complicate things. To tackle these problems, we need to use some tailored strategies to make sure our food stays safe and nutritious:

Challenges

Extreme Heat: High temperatures accelerate food spoilage and nutrient loss, making it difficult to preserve perishable items without refrigeration.

Water Scarcity: Limited water availability restricts water-intensive preservation methods like canning and fermentation, making it challenging to maintain traditional preservation practices.

Energy Dependence: Cooling and refrigeration systems are essential but energy-intensive, which can be problematic in areas with unreliable or expensive electricity.

Low Humidity: While low humidity is beneficial for drying, it can lead to over-drying, causing foods to become brittle and lose quality.

Pest Infestations: Extreme heat can drive pests indoors, potentially contaminating stored foods.

Strategies

Solar-Powered Preservation: Utilize solar dehydrators and solar-powered refrigeration to maximize abundant sunlight while reducing energy costs.

Water-Efficient Methods: Dry curing, smoking, and vacuum sealing are the most effective methods for minimizing water use while effectively preserving food.

Cool Storage Solutions: Explore underground storage or use clay pot coolers (Zeer pots) to maintain lower temperatures without relying heavily on electricity.

Natural Pest Control: Implement natural pest deterrents, such as diatomaceous earth and neem oil, to protect stored foods without chemical treatments.

Community Education: Provide training on adapting traditional methods and using modern technologies suitable for arid climates, helping communities maintain effective preservation practices.

Improve Airflow in Drying: Use wind or shaded drying areas to prevent over-drying while ensuring foods are adequately preserved.

Food preservation in arid and desert climates requires innovative approaches that leverage natural resources while addressing the challenges of extreme heat and water scarcity. By implementing solar-powered solutions, water-efficient methods, and natural pest control, communities can effectively preserve food and enhance food security in these challenging environments.

Cold and Temperate Climates

Cold and temperate climates present their own challenges for keeping food fresh. Seasonal changes, shorter growing seasons, and the need for solid storage options during long winters can make it tricky to preserve food effectively.

Challenges

Seasonal Availability: Short growing seasons mean that large quantities of food must be preserved quickly to last through the winter, requiring significant storage space and resources.

Temperature Control: While cold temperatures aid in natural refrigeration, fluctuating temperatures can cause issues such as freezing and cracking of canned goods or inconsistent fermentation results.

Energy Costs: Heating is often needed to maintain optimal conditions for certain preservation methods, such as fermentation and drying, which can increase energy costs, especially during winter.

Pest Infestations: Cold weather can drive pests indoors, where they might infest stored foods, particularly grains and root vegetables.

Strategies

Cold Storage Optimization: Utilize natural cold storage options like root cellars or insulated pantries to take advantage of naturally cool temperatures, reducing the need for artificial refrigeration.

Freezing Techniques: Using the cold climate to freeze foods can be an efficient preservation method when energy costs are lower or outdoor freezing is possible.

Canning and Jarring: Take advantage of the cool climate by focusing on canning and jarring, which can be stored in cool environments without the risk of spoilage. Ensure proper insulation to avoid freezing.

Fermentation Control: Use insulated fermentation vessels or temperature-controlled environments to ensure consistent fermentation, even in fluctuating temperatures.

Energy-Efficient Preservation: To reduce energy costs during preservation, invest in energy-efficient equipment for heating and drying, such as low-energy dehydrators or insulated drying rooms.

Pest Management: Implement pest control measures such as regular monitoring, airtight containers, and natural deterrents to protect stored foods from infestation during winter.

In colder and temperate regions, keeping food fresh takes some smart planning to tackle the ups and downs of seasonal availability and temperature changes. By making the most of cold storage, using energy-saving techniques, and managing the preservation conditions carefully, communities can maintain a steady food supply all year round.

Polar and Subpolar Climates

Polar and subpolar climates are known for their intense cold, lengthy winters, and short growing seasons, meaning preserving food is crucial for survival. These tough conditions bring about specific challenges that require tailored strategies to tackle.

Challenges

Extreme Cold: While the cold can naturally preserve food, it also presents risks such as freezing and cracking containers, making storing certain preserved foods difficult.

Short Growing Season: The very limited growing season means that fresh produce is only available for a short time, necessitating the preservation of large quantities of food to last through the long winter.

Limited Energy Resources: In remote areas, access to consistent energy supplies can be limited, making reliance on energy-intensive preservation methods like freezing or canning difficult.

Transportation Barriers: The remote and harsh conditions often make transporting preserved foods and supplies challenging and expensive, limiting access to preservation materials and equipment.

Strategies

Natural Freezing: Use extreme cold to freeze foods naturally. This method can be particularly effective for long-term preservation without energy-intensive freezers.

Root Cellars and Snow Storage: Construct insulated root cellars or use snow and ice storage methods to keep food cool and preserved throughout the year, leveraging the natural cold environment.

Drying in Controlled Environments: Dry foods indoors using controlled environments to prevent over-drying and brittleness, which can occur in extremely cold and dry conditions.

Fermentation in Insulated Spaces: Conduct fermentation in insulated or temperature-controlled spaces to maintain consistent temperatures, ensuring successful fermentation even in freezing conditions.

Smoking and Curing: Smoking and dry curing, which require minimal energy and are well-suited to cold, dry climates, are recommended to preserve meats and fish for long-term storage.

Community Collaboration: Share resources within communities, such as communal preservation facilities or shared access to energy-efficient equipment, to maximize efficiency and reduce individual costs.

Utilize Indigenous Knowledge: Incorporate traditional preservation methods used by Indigenous populations, such as air-drying fish or fermenting in natural cold environments, adapted to extreme conditions over generations.

Keeping food fresh is important for surviving long winters and short growing seasons in polar and subpolar regions. By taking advantage of the natural cold, using time-tested methods, and improving storage options, communities can ensure a steady and reliable food supply all year round, even in tough conditions.

By recognizing the unique challenges of different climates and using these strategies, you can boost food security and guarantee access to safe, nutritious food all year. Adapting and getting creative with these approaches will be crucial for tackling preservation issues.

Wrapping it Up...

This chapter explored different food preservation techniques to keep food fresh and healthy for longer. The secret to successful food preservation is knowing your food well and picking the right method to keep it safe and tasty. With these tips, you can live a more sustainable and resilient lifestyle.

Key Points

Food Preservation: Extends shelf life, reduces waste, and ensures food security by having a reliable food supply. Different methods work best for different types of foods.
DIY vs. Store-Bought: DIY food preservation saves money and encourages self-sufficiency but takes time and effort. Store-bought foods provide convenience and variety but can be pricey.
Picking the Best Preservation Method: Your fresh foods, dietary habits, and taste preferences will guide you in selecting the perfect DIY food preservation methods.
Nutritional Impact: Preservation can affect nutrient retention differently, with freezing and freeze-drying being the best for keeping nutrients intact.
For Beginners: Start simple, invest wisely, preserve in batches, learn from others, keep track of costs, and stay organized.
Seasonal Planning: Planning ahead ensures you have a variety of tasty and nutritious foods all year round, making you more resilient and self-sufficient.

Online Resources

- National Center for Home Food Preservation (USDA): Comprehensive guides on food preservation techniques, including considerations for different climates and environmental conditions. https://nchfp.uga.edu/

- Food and Agriculture Organization of the United Nations (FAO): Global resources on food preservation methods suited to various climates, with an emphasis on developing countries and local adaptations. https://www.fao.org/home/en/

- National Institute of Food and Agriculture (NIFA): Research and resources on food preservation, including how to adapt practices for different climatic conditions. https://www.nifa.usda.gov/

- National Sustainable Agriculture Coalition (NSAC): Advocacy for sustainable food systems, including preservation techniques adapted to various climates. https://sustainableagriculture.net/

- Slow Food International: Promotes traditional food preservation methods that are climate-specific, helping communities preserve local food cultures. https://www.slowfood.com/

- The Ecological Farming Association: Resources and training on ecological farming practices, including food preservation methods tailored to specific climates. https://eco-farm.org/

- Solar Cookers International: Promotes solar cooking and food preservation techniques suitable for sunny, dry climates. https://www.solarcookers.org/

5

Essential Foods

Honey found in ancient Egyptian tombs is still edible after 3,000 years—talk about an essential food!

When storing food for the long haul, it's critical to pinpoint the must-have items that will help you keep a healthy and diverse diet. You want to strike a good balance of macronutrients and micronutrients by including all the essential food groups while also considering taste, nutrition, and how food affects our mood. In this chapter, we will put together all we have learned in previous chapters to compile an essential foods list that will be the basis for your long-term *Food Survival Plan*.

A Quick Recap

Let's quickly recap the key components we have learned that are needed for a nutritious and sustainable essential foods list.

Food Groups

Include a mix of food groups offering balanced nutrition. If your diet is inadequate, consider taking vitamin and mineral supplements.

Carbohydrates: Grains & starches form the backbone of any stockpile, providing essential carbohydrates for energy and satiety while offering long shelf lives and versatility in meals.

Proteins: Crucial for muscle maintenance, energy, and overall health, making it important to include both animal and plant-based protein sources that store well and are easy to prepare.

Fats & Oils: Vital for absorbing key vitamins and providing long-lasting energy, so storing shelf-stable oils and fats is key to maintaining a balanced diet.

Fruits & Vegetables: Supply critical vitamins and minerals necessary for immune function and overall health, and preserving them through canning, dehydrating, or freeze-drying ensures long-term availability.

Dairy: Provide calcium, protein, and fats, and their powdered or shelf-stable forms are perfect for adding to meals when fresh products aren't available.

Food Group Ratios

Aim for a good balance of carbs, proteins, fats, oils, dairy, and other essentials. Focus on foods that are nutrient-dense and also have a long shelf life. For long-term food storage, you'll want to lean towards a lower carb and higher nutrition ratio than what you'd typically store for shorter periods. This way, you'll have a solid stash that keeps you healthy over time. Here's a solid ratio you can use for your long-term food storage:

Carbohydrates	30-40%
Proteins	15-25%
Fats & Oils	15-20%
Fruits and Vegetables	15-20%
Dairy	10-15%

In a later chapter, we will apply these ratios to your essential foods to calculate food storage quantities for your stockpile.

Water for Hydration

The most crucial element of any stockpile is water. It is needed for drinking and cooking, hygiene, and maintaining health during emergencies. Have at least 1 gallon per person per day.

Dietary Requirements

Consider any special dietary needs, such as allergies, intolerances, or dietary preferences (e.g., gluten-free, vegetarian).

Superfoods

Packed with nutrients, superfoods like blueberries, spinach, quinoa, and almonds contain vitamins and minerals that can help keep you healthy when fresh produce is scarce.

Caloric Needs

Getting a grip on your calorie needs is important for keeping your energy up and staying healthy during long-term emergencies:

Total Caloric Needs: Ensure your food list meets the total caloric needs of each person in your household. Consider both normal daily activities and more physically demanding situations.

High-Calorie Foods: Include calorie-dense foods like peanut butter, nuts, seeds, energy bars, and dried fruits. These foods are essential for providing quick, sustained energy in a compact form.

Taste and Comfort Foods

Don't underestimate the importance of taste and comfort:

Herbs & Spices: Enhances food flavor and helps prevent palate fatigue, making them essential for maintaining variety and enjoyment in your diet.

Condiments and Sauces: Add richness and flavor to meals, helping to elevate simple dishes and provide much-needed variety in a survival situation.

Comfort Foods: Boosts morale and provides a sense of normalcy, offering psychological relief during stressful times.

Beverages: These should offer both hydration and comfort, which is important for maintaining physical and mental well-being in long-term scenarios.

Download The Free Spreadsheet

As we progress, you'll encounter a few fill-in tables designed for you to input information relevant to your situation. I've created a free downloadable spreadsheet that includes all the fill-in templates and extra resources like the *Prepper's Food Survival Calculator* to assist you. For those of you who are old school, you can write your information in the fill-in tables throughout the book.

Save a Copy of the Spreadsheet

You will need to download and save a copy of the spreadsheet to input data and edit tables. Here is how you do that:

Step 1: Access the Spreadsheet

Copy this link into your browser:

htttps://docs.google.com/spreadsheets/d/1jjTtTd89kzqi_Vb3rxJly4jpdisl5dk2eTlBb9auTJg/edit?usp=sharing

or Scan the QR Code:

- This will open the Google Sheets file in a new browser tab. You do not need a Google account to use Google Sheets.

- If you have a Google account and want to use Google Sheets:

- Click on File > Make a copy to save your own version.

- You can then edit and save changes directly in Google Sheets.

Step 2: For other File Types

- Once the spreadsheet opens, click on File in the top menu.

- Select Download from the dropdown menu.

- Choose your preferred format:
  - Microsoft Excel (.xlsx) for use in Excel.
  - PDF if you want a read-only version.
  - CSV for use in other spreadsheet software (like LibreOffice Calc).

If you have any suggestions or feedback on the spreadsheet, you can email me at andrewrainesauthor@gmail.com.

Putting Together Your Essential Foods

You can now start making your essential foods list. These include your DIY Preserved foods, Store-Bought options, and Taste and Comfort foods.

Your DIY Preserved Foods

Let's start with your your DIY Preserved Foods. As we discussed in the DIY Food Preservation chapter, these will depend on things like your fresh food sources, shelf life, storage space, and tools:

	Foods
Water Bath Canning (High-acid foods)	
Pressure Canning (Low-acid foods)	
Dehydration	
Fermentation	
Freezing	
Freeze Drying	
Vacuum Sealing	
Salting/ Curing	
Sugaring	
Smoking	
Pickling	

Store-Bought Long Life Foods

Your store-bought foods list will likely include long-life store-bought foods to complement your DIY preserved foods. Here are some example foods from each major food group:

	Food Item	Shelf Life
Carbs / Grains	Rice	25-30 years
	Oats	2-5 years
	Pasta	8-10 years
	Quinoa	2-3 years
	Cornmeal	2-3 years
	Barley	2-3 years
	Flour	1-2 years
	Couscous	2-3 years
Proteins	Canned Tuna, Salmon, Sardines	2-5 years
	Canned Chicken or Turkey	2-5 years
	Canned Ham, Spam, Corned Beef	3-5 years
	Canned Beans	2-5 years
	Dried Beans (lentils, split peas)	10-30 years
	Peanut Butter	1-2 years
	Freeze-Dried Meat	15-25 years
	Beef Jerky	1-2 years
	MREs (Meals Ready to Eat)	5-10 years
Fats & Oils	Vegetable Oil	1-2 years
	Olive Oil	1-2 years
	Coconut Oil	2-3 years
	Ghee (Clarified Butter)	2-5 years
	Nuts and Seeds	1-2 years
Fruits & Vegetables	Canned Fruits	1-2 years
	Canned Vegetables	2-5 years
	Canned Tomatoes	1-2 years
	Dried Fruits	1-2 years
	Freeze-Dried Vegetables	15-25 years
	Freeze-Dried Fruits	15-25 years
	Sauerkraut & Pickles	1-2 years
Dairy	Powdered Milk	20-25 years
	Evaporated Milk	1-2 years
	Sweetened Condensed Milk	2-5 years
	Shelf-Stable UHT Milk	6-12 months

Example Essentials Foods

Here is an example list of essential foods, which combines DIY preserved and store-bought foods:

	Food	Calories per Serving	Nutrients	Notes
Carbs / Grains	Rice	102 / oz	High in carbs	Long shelf life; versatile.
	Pasta	105 / oz	High in carbs	Easy to store and cook
	Oats	110 / oz	Fiber, iron, & protein	For breakfast & baking
	Corn meal	103 / oz	High in carbs, protein	For cornbread & polenta
	Flour	103 / oz	Carbs, protein	All-purpose flour
	Wheat	96 / oz	High in fiber	Long shelf life, versatile
	Quinoa	106 / oz	Protein & amino acids	Grain with a long shelf life.
Proteins	Canned Beans (DIY)	120 / ¼ jar	Protein, fiber, & iron	Black beans, chickpeas
	Canned Meat (DIY)	75 / ¼ jar	High in protein	Chicken, spam
	Tuna (3 oz can)	75 / can	Protein & omega-3s	Easy to store, versatile
	Dried Lentils	170 / ¼ cup	Protein, fiber, iron	Quick cooking.
	Peanut Butter	190 / 2 tbsp	Protein & healthy fats	Long shelf life, energy-dense
	Beef Jerky	85 / oz	High in protein	Shelf-stable snack.
	Freeze-Dried Beef	70 / oz	Iron, zinc, and Vit B	25 year shelf life, no fridge
	MRE	300 / ¼ MRE	Balanced Macro	Meal kits, shelf life of 3-5 yrs
Fats & Oils	Vegetable Oil	120 / tbsp	High in healthy fats	Cooking & baking.
	Olive Oil	120 / tbsp	Mono fats, antioxidants	Adds flavor and versatile use.
	Nuts & Seeds	160 / oz	Healthy fats, protein	Great for snacking
Fruits & Vegetables	Dried Fruits	140 / ¼ cup	Natural sugars, fiber	Raisins, apricots, apples
	Canned Fruit (DIY)	70 / ¼ jar	Vitamin C, fiber	Pineapple, peaches, mixed
	Canned Vegetables (DIY)	40 / ¼ jar	Vitamins A, C, fiber	Corn, green beans, carrots
	Freeze-Dried Veggies	30 / 1 oz	Retains nutrients, fiber	Peas, corn, broccoli
	Sauerkraut & Pickles (DIY)	25 / ½ jar	Probiotics, vitamin C	Adds Variety
Dairy	Powdered Milk	130 / 3 tbsp	Calcium & protein.	Long shelf life
	Shelf-Stable Milk	150 / cup	Calcium & protein.	Alternative to fresh milk
	Shelf-Stable Cheese	110 / oz	Calcium & protein.	Processed & hard cheese
Water	Stored Water	0 / 1 cup	Essential for hydration	1 gal per person per day

Your Essential Foods

You can start your personalized essential foods list by adding your DIY Preserved, Store-bought, and Taste and Comfort Foods. Be sure to include a variety of food groups that support a healthy lifestyle while catering to your household's tastes, well-being, and dietary needs.

Your Essential Foods list is not fixed. Like your overall *Food Survival Plan*, it's important to be flexible and adapt to changing situations. As long as you maintain a good variety of foods across different food groups, making adjustments is perfectly fine.

I've compiled a detailed list of common preserved foods and their calorie counts per serving in the spreadsheet and A. This information is valuable later when we look into calculating your food storage quantities.

If you can't find something on the list, just check out the website for more information on common foods.

	Food	Calories / Serving Size	Notes
Carbs / Grains			
Proteins			
Fats & Oils			
Fruits & Vegs			
Dairy			
Water			

Taste and Comfort Foods

These are the foods that don't fall into one of the major food groups but are important for variety and morale in long-term food storage.

Here are some example foods:

	Food Item	Shelf Life
Herbs & Spices	Salt	Indefinite
	Black Pepper	2-3 years
	Chili Powder	2-3 years
	Garlic Powder	2-4 years
	Dried Herbs	2-3 years
Sauces & Condiments	Ketchup	1-2 years
	Mustard	1-2 years
	Hot Sauce	2-5 years
	Mayonnaise	6-12 months
	Salad Dressing	6-12 months
	BBQ Sauce	1-2 years
	Vinegar	Indefinite
	Soy Sauce	2-3 years
	Worcestershire Sauce	2-3 years
Comfort Foods	Chocolate Bars	1-2 years
	Candy	2-3 years
	Granola/Protein Bars	1-2 years
	Ramen Noodles	2-5 years
	Crackers	1-2 years
	Popcorn Kernels	10-15 years
Beverages	Coffee (instant, ground)	2-20 years
	Tea (tea bags)	1-2 years
	Cocoa Powder	2-3 years
	Fruit Juice (shelf-stable)	6-12 months
	Powdered Drink Mixes	2-5 years
Other	Sugar	Indefinite
	Honey	Indefinite
	Molasses	1-2 years
	Baking Soda & Baking Powder	1-2 years
	Yeast	2-5 years

You can now add your taste and comfort foods to the table below:

	Food Item	Shelf Life
Herbs & Spices		
Sauces & Condiments		
Comfort Foods		
Beverages		
Other		

Non Food Items

When preparing your long-term storage, thinking beyond just food is important. You must also stock up on non-food essentials vital for survival, health, and keeping your supplies in good shape. Here's a handy list of must-have non-food items to keep in mind:

Water

Bottled Water: At least 1 gallon per person daily for drinking, cooking, and hygiene.

Water Filters/Purifiers: Portable filters or purifiers to make water from natural sources safe to drink.

Water Storage Containers: Large barrels, water bricks, or collapsible containers for bulk storage.

Water Purification Tablets: Chlorine or iodine tablets for quick water treatment.

Cooking and Fuel

Camping Stove or Rocket Stove: This is for cooking when conventional stoves aren't usable.

Propane or Butane: Fuel for portable stoves, stored in sufficient quantities.

Wood, Charcoal, or Fire Starters: For cooking over a fire in an emergency.

Matches, Lighters, or Fire-Starting Kits: Waterproof options for reliability.

Manual Can Opener: For opening canned goods when electricity isn't available.

Cookware: Durable pots, pans, and utensils suited for outdoor or off-grid cooking.

Hygiene and Sanitation

Toilet Paper: Stored in bulk for long-term use.

Hand Sanitizer and Soap: Essential for maintaining personal hygiene.

Baby Wipes or Wet Wipes: Useful for cleaning when water is limited.

Feminine Hygiene Products: Pads, tampons, or menstrual cups for women.

Disposable Gloves: For handling waste or contaminated items.

Bleach or Disinfectant: For sanitation and cleaning purposes.

Trash Bags: Heavy-duty bags for waste disposal or emergency sanitation.

Medical and First Aid

First Aid Kit: Basic kit with bandages, antiseptic wipes, gauze, and pain relievers.

Prescription Medications: Extra supply of necessary medications, if possible.

Over-the-counter medications: Pain relievers, antacids, antihistamines, and cold/flu medicine.

Multivitamins: To supplement potential nutrient gaps in the diet.

Thermometer: For checking fevers and monitoring health.

Personal Protective Equipment (PPE): Masks, face shields, and gloves for pandemics or hazardous situations.

Lighting and Power

Flashlights: Battery-powered or hand-crank flashlights for lighting.

Headlamps: Useful for hands-free lighting in the dark.

Extra Batteries: For flashlights, radios, and other battery-powered devices.

Solar Charger: To keep electronic devices like phones and radios charged.

Candles and Matches: These are for backup lighting options.

Communication

Hand-Crank or Battery-Powered Radio: This is for receiving emergency alerts and news.

Two-Way Radios: For communication within the household or with neighbors.

Whistle: For signaling in case of an emergency.

External Battery Packs: For recharging phones or small electronics.

Personal Care Items

Toothpaste and Toothbrushes: Basic dental hygiene supplies.

Shampoo and Conditioner: Store extra for maintaining hygiene.

Razors and Shaving Cream: For shaving needs.

Deodorant: An important hygiene item for longer-term comfort.

Tools and Repair

Multi-Tool or Swiss Army Knife: Versatile tool for repairs and various tasks.

Duct Tape: For temporary repairs, sealing containers, or creating shelter.

Tarps and Rope: For shelter-building or covering supplies.

Plastic Sheeting: For weatherproofing or emergency sheltering.

Nails, Screws, and Hammer: For basic repair work or fortification.

Firearms, Ammunition, and Self-Defense

Firearms and Ammunition: For self-defense or hunting, if appropriate.

Pepper Spray or Personal Alarms: Non-lethal self-defense options.

Security System: Motion-sensor alarms or cameras for home protection.

Comfort and Morale Items

Books, Games, and Puzzles: For entertainment and mental well-being.

Paper and Pens: For taking notes, making lists, or maintaining records.

Playing Cards or Board Games: For maintaining morale during long emergencies.

Storage and Organization

Storage Bins or Buckets: For organizing food and supplies.

Vacuum-Seal Bags: For extending shelf life and protecting dry goods.

Mylar Bags and Oxygen Absorbers: For long-term storage of dry foods.

Labels and Markers: For labeling containers, dates, and expiration info.

Emergency Cash and Important Documents

Cash: Small denominations for emergency purchases when electronic payments are impossible.

Copies of Important Documents: IDs, insurance, medical records, and emergency contacts in a waterproof container.

Seeds for Gardening

Heirloom Seeds: For growing vegetables, herbs, and fruits to supplement long-term food storage.

Wrapping it Up...

In this chapter, you've learned how to compile a list of essential foods that align with your nutritional goals, calorie requirements, and personal preferences. Maintaining a balanced variety of food groups is important to ensure your household stays healthy over time.

Next, we'll explore your food stockpile, including how to store and manage it, and later, we will learn how to determine the amount of food you need.

> **Key Points**
>
> **Nutrition and Calories:** Important to eat healthy and maintain energy.
> **Food Groups:** Include a good variety from the five major food groups.
> **Water:** Have at least 1 gallon per person per day.
> **Preserved Foods:** A mix of store-bought and DIY preserved foods.
> **Taste and Comfort:** Foods that contribute to positive mood and morale.
> **Your Essential Food List:** The basis for your long-term stored food.
> **Non-Food Items:** Valuable items to include for the long term.

Online Resources

- USDA FoodData Central: Detailed nutritional information for various food items.

- USDA MyPlate: Information on nutrition and healthy eating. It offers a variety of tools, guidelines, and resources to help individuals and families make healthier food choices.

- National Institutes of Health (NIH) - A resource for food, calories, and health information. Includes tools for calorie counting, meal planning, and dietary guidelines. https://www.nutrition.gov/

- The Academy of Nutrition and Dietetics (EatRight): Provides nutrition and diet advice, including detailed guides on calories, macronutrients, and portion control. https://www.eatright.org/

- EatByDate: Provides information on food shelf life and

tips on managing special dietary needs within a stockpile. https://eatbydate.com/

- <u>CDC Emergency</u> "Emergency Preparedness and Response": information on preparing for emergencies, including recommendations for essential supplies to maintain health and safety during disasters.

6

STOCKPILE AND PANTRY

The world's largest pantry is a U.S. government facility storing over 2.7 billion pounds of food.

Figuring out where to get your food and how you like to preserve it is just the beginning. Stocking up on food is important for preparing and ensuring you and your family have enough to eat during tough times. A well-organized and fully stocked stockpile and pantry give you peace of mind, helping you handle unexpected events like natural disasters, economic struggles, or personal challenges.

Difference Between Stockpile and Pantry

In the prepper community, a stockpile keeps individuals or families going for a long time during emergencies, disasters, etc. A pantry, on the other hand, is more about everyday needs and quick access. But it's not set in stone—people often use the terms interchangeably in prepper discussions.

Optimizing Storage Conditions

Keeping your stockpile and pantry neat and organized is important for keeping your food fresh and safe. You can avoid spoilage, contamination, and nutrient loss with simple tips and tricks. Here are some handy suggestions for setting up the perfect storage conditions to ensure your food stays in top shape:

Temperature Control

Cool Environment

Ideal Temperature: Keep your pantry consistently between 50°F and 70°F. Avoid areas that are subject to extreme temperature fluctuations.

Thermometer: Monitor the temperature in your pantry with a thermometer. Place it in a visible location and check it regularly to ensure it stays within the ideal range.

Avoid Heat Sources

Away from Appliances: Store pantry items away from heat-producing appliances like ovens, stoves, and dishwashers.

Sunlight: Avoid direct sunlight, which can increase temperature and degrade food quality. Use curtains or blinds to block sunlight from windows near the pantry.

Humidity Control

Low Humidity

Ideal Humidity Level: Maintain a humidity level of 50% or lower to prevent mold growth and spoilage. High humidity can cause dry goods to absorb moisture and spoil faster.

Dehumidifier: Use a dehumidifier in areas with high humidity to keep moisture levels in check. This is especially crucial in basements or regions with naturally high humidity.

Moisture Barriers

Airtight Containers: Store dry goods like grains, flour, and sugar in airtight containers to protect them from moisture. Also helps prevent pest infestations.

Silica Gel Packs: Place silica gel packs in containers or on pantry shelves to absorb excess moisture and keep the environment dry.

Light Control

Dark Environment

Light Exposure: Minimize light exposure, especially direct sunlight, which can degrade the quality of certain foods, such as oils, spices, and canned goods.

Opaque Containers: Use opaque or tinted containers for items sensitive to light to protect them from light exposure.

Lighting Solutions

Low-Heat Lighting: Install low-heat, energy-efficient lighting, such as LED lights, in your pantry. Avoid incandescent bulbs, which produce heat and can raise the pantry's temperature.

Motion Sensors: Consider using motion-sensor lighting to reduce the time lights are on in the pantry, helping maintain a cooler environment.

Pest Control

Preventing Infestations

Airtight Containers: Store all dry goods in airtight containers to prevent pests like ants, moths, and rodents from accessing food.

Sealing Cracks: Inspect your pantry for cracks or holes where pests could enter and seal them with caulk or weather stripping.

Regular Cleaning

Routine Cleaning: Regularly clean shelves, containers, and floors to remove crumbs and spills that attract pests. Use a vacuum cleaner to reach corners and crevices.

Natural Deterrents: Place natural pest deterrents like bay leaves, cloves, or lavender sachets on pantry shelves to repel insects.

Air Circulation

Ventilation

Proper Airflow: Ensure adequate airflow in your pantry to prevent the buildup of stale air and moisture. Good ventilation helps keep the environment dry and reduces the risk of mold and mildew.

Ventilation Fans: Install a small ventilation fan or exhaust fan if your pantry is enclosed and lacks natural airflow.

Organized Layout

Spacing Items: Avoid overcrowding shelves. Leave some space between items to allow air to circulate freely around them. Also makes it easier to see and access items.

Open Shelving: Consider using open shelving units instead of closed cabinets to improve air circulation.

Root Cellaring

The traditional method of food preservation involves storing fruits and vegetables in a cool, humid, and dark environment to extend their shelf life. It takes advantage of natural refrigeration and humidity to keep food fresh for extended periods without the need for electricity or modern refrigeration.

Monitoring and Maintenance

Routine Checks: Schedule regular inspections of your pantry to check for signs of spoilage, pests, and other issues. A monthly or bi-monthly check is recommended.

Inventory Management: Regularly update your inventory list as you add or use items. This helps maintain accurate records and simplifies the rotation process.

Ongoing Maintenance: Wipe down shelves and containers as needed to prevent dust and grime buildup. Promptly clean up any spills to avoid attracting pests.

Deep Cleaning: Perform a deep cleaning at least twice a year. Remove all items, clean shelves, and containers, and check for expired or spoiled items.

Storage in Small Spaces

If you're living in an apartment, you've got to get a bit creative with your space and stay organized. Here's how to maximize your food storage:

Prioritize Essentials

Focus on compact, long-lasting items:

Dried Goods: Rice, beans, pasta, and grains.

Canned Goods: Vegetables, fruits, meats, and soups.

Dehydrated/Frozen-Dried Foods: Lightweight and space-efficient.

Nuts and Seeds: High in nutrients, easy to store.

Utilize Vertical Space

Shelving: Add shelves to unused walls for extra storage.

Overhead Storage: Use hanging racks or shelves in the kitchen.

Stackable Containers: Optimize cupboard space with stackable bins.

Optimize Underutilized Areas

Under-Bed Storage: Store items in low-profile bins.

Closets: Use shelves or hanging organizers for food storage.

Cabinet Doors: Install racks for spices and small items.

Multi-Functional Furniture

Storage Ottomans and Benches: Store food discreetly.

Under-Counter Cabinets: Use for additional storage space.

Compact Appliances

Small Freezer: Provides extra space for frozen foods.

Compact Dehydrator: Store easily when not in use.

Vacuum Sealer: Saves space by compressing foods.

Stay Organized

Clear Containers: Easy to see contents.

Labels: Mark contents and expiration dates.

Inventory: Track your stockpile to avoid waste.

Think Outside the Kitchen

Bookshelves: Use in other rooms for storage.

Laundry Area: Add a shelf or bins for extra supplies.

Waterproofing Your Food Storage

Waterproofing your food storage is crucial to prevent moisture-related spoilage, mold, and contamination. Here are key strategies to keep your food safe and dry:

Use Airtight Containers

Plastic Bins & Glass Jars: Store food in airtight plastic bins or glass jars with tight-sealing lids to keep out moisture.

Vacuum-Sealed Bags: Vacuum-sealed dry goods to remove air and moisture, extending shelf life.

Add Desiccants

Silica Gel Packs: Place silica gel packs inside containers to absorb moisture.

DIY Desiccants: Use dried rice or salt in small bags to control humidity in storage areas.

Waterproof Storage Areas

Raised Shelving: Store food on raised shelves to protect from flooding or leaks.

Sealed Rooms: Use waterproof paint or sealant in storage rooms to prevent water seepage.

Use Waterproof Bags and Wraps

Mylar Bags: Store foods in Mylar bags for a moisture-resistant barrier.

Plastic Wrap: Wrap items in plastic or foil before storing them to add protection.

Monitor and Maintain

Regular Inspections: Check storage areas regularly for moisture or leaks and address issues immediately.

Replace Desiccants: Refresh desiccants periodically to maintain their effectiveness.

Keeping your food supply safe from moisture is critical. You can do this by using airtight containers, throwing in some desiccants, making sure your storage areas are secure, and doing regular check-ups. This way, your food will stay fresh and good to eat for a longer time.

Food Storage Containers

It's important to store your food correctly to keep it fresh and safe. Choosing suitable containers for different foods can greatly affect how long they last. Store-bought foods with sealed containers like cans or jars can be left as is while noting the used-by dates.

Here is a table of various food container options, their benefits, materials, and sizes:

	Uses	Material	Sizes	Storage Duration
Freezer Bags	Frozen fruits, vegetables, meats	Heavy-duty plastic	1 quart up to 1 gal	Short to Medium
Airtight Plastic Containers	Dry goods - flour, sugar, grains, pasta	BPA-free plastic	1 quart up to 20 gal	Short to Medium
Glass Food Storage Containers	Leftovers, prepared meals, snacks	Tempered glass	Small 1-2 cups Medium 3-4 cups Large 6-8 cups	Short to Medium
Mason Jars	Spices, herbs, nuts, seeds, home-canned goods	Tempered glass	Half-pint up to half-gal	Short to Medium
Vacuum-Sealed Bags	Meats, cheeses, vegetables, prepared meals	Multi-layer plastic with textured side	Rolls or pre-cut sizes Pint to gal	Short to Medium
Canned Food	Canned beans, vegetables, fruits, meats	Tin-coated steel or aluminum	Small 8 oz Medium 15 oz Large 28 oz	Medium to Long
Plastic Storage Bins with Lids	Bulk items and larger food quantities	Durable plastic with snap-on or locking lids	Medium 10-15 gal Large 20-30 gal	Medium to Long
Food-Grade Buckets	Bulk storage of dry goods - grains, beans, pasta	High-density polyethylene (HDPE)	2 gal, 5 gal and 6 gal	Long Term
Metal Cans (#10 Cans)	Freeze-dried and dehydrated foods	Tin-coated steel or aluminum	Approx 109 fluid oz	Long Term
Mylar Bags	Long-term storage of dry foods	Polyester film with metallic coating	1 quart up to 5 gal	Long Term

Containers for Your Essential Foods

Here's a blank table where you can add the container type to your own essential foods:

	Foods	Size	Storage Location
Airtight Plastic Containers			
Food-Grade Buckets			
Mylar Bags with Oxygen Absorbers			
Mason Jars			
Glass Food Storage Containers			
Vacuum-Sealed Bags			
Plastic Storage Bins with Lids			
Metal Cans (#10 Cans)			

Organizing Your Pantry and Stockpile

Organizing your pantry helps ensure you have all the necessary food items in case of an emergency. It also makes it easier to find what you need and keeps your food fresh. Here, we look at different methods of organizing your food storage to save space, be more efficient, and prevent food wastage.

Categorize by Food Group

This method allows you to assess whether you have a balanced diet and enough variety in each category to sustain you over time. Grouping by food type also makes it easier to locate specific ingredients when planning meals or rotating stock:

Grains & Starches: Rice, pasta, oats, flour, quinoa

Proteins: Canned meats, beans, lentils, nuts, protein powders

Fats & Oils: Olive oil, coconut oil, ghee, canned fish in oil

Fruits & Vegetables: Canned fruits and vegetables, freeze-dried or dehydrated produce

Dairy: Powdered milk, shelf-stable milk, canned cheese

Herbs & Spices: Dried herbs, spices, seasoning mixes

Condiments & Sauces: Soy Sauce, Vinegar, Hot Sauce, Ketchup and Mustard

Comfort Foods: Chocolates, candy, snacks, instant desserts

Beverages: Instant coffee, tea, electrolyte powders

3-Tier Food Storage Method

The 3-Tier Food Storage System is a handy way to keep food organized and your kitchen running smoothly. It's a favorite among preppers, homesteaders, and anyone who wants to ensure they're stocked.

This method divides food storage into three levels. The top tier is for your go-to items, like snacks and quick meals you grab all the time. The middle tier is for stuff you use regularly but not every day, like grains and canned goods. The bottom tier is where you stash your long-term supplies, like bulk items or seasonal ingredients.

This setup saves space and makes it super easy to find what you need when you need it. Plus, it helps cut down on food waste since everything is visible and within reach.

Tier 1: Short-Term (up to 3 Months)

Tier 1 is about prepping for short-term emergencies lasting up to 3 months. This tier focuses on stocking up on perishable items like fresh produce, dairy products, bread, eggs, and ready-to-eat meals that you use regularly. Rotating these items often is important to keep them fresh and avoid spoilage. With a few weeks' supply of these essential perishable foods, you'll be ready to meet your family's immediate nutritional needs in case of unexpected short-term situations.

Tier 2: Intermediate-Term (3 to 12 Months)

Tier 2 is your backup plan for when things get rough for a more extended period, like when the power goes out for a while or the economy takes a hit. It's all about stocking up on non-perishable items that can last a long time without refrigeration. Think canned goods, dried foods, and pantry staples like pasta, rice, beans, and powdered milk. Keep these items in a cool, dark spot, and make sure to use up the older stuff first. Having a few months' supply of these basics means you'll always have some good, nutritious food on hand, which can help you avoid frequent trips to the grocery store and give you peace of mind during extended emergencies.

Tier 3: Long-Term (12 months or more)

Tier 3 is about ensuring you have enough food to last through major emergencies or significant changes in your life. This tier includes foods that can last a really long time, like Freeze-Dried foods, Dehydrated foods, and bulk grains stored in special bags with oxygen absorbers. If you store these foods properly in a cool, dark place, they can stay good for years, giving you a reliable source of food when fresh options aren't available. A solid long-term food storage plan means you can ensure your family has enough to eat, no matter how long or serious the situation is.

Benefits of the 3-Tier Food Storage Method

Comprehensive Preparedness: Covers short-term, intermediate-term, and long-term food storage needs, ensuring readiness for various emergencies.

Systematic Management: Helps stockpile management and rotation, maintaining freshness and nutritional value.

Flexibility: It is adaptable to different scenarios, from immediate disruptions like power outages to prolonged crises like economic downturns.

Reduced Waste: Regular rotation and inventory management practices minimize food waste.

Nutritional Assurance: Ensures a balanced diet by incorporating a variety of foods with different shelf lives.

Peace of Mind: Provides confidence and security, knowing you have a reliable food supply for your family.

Sustainability: A sustainable and resilient lifestyle is supported by planning and maintaining a long-term food storage strategy.

The 3-Tier Food Storage Method is a smart way to set up a solid food storage system. By dividing your food supplies into short-term, intermediate-term, and long-term storage, you can be ready for anything. This method helps you stay organized and ensure a well-rounded diet, even in emergencies.

Organize by Usage

Another practical way to group food is by how you plan to use it:

Meal Components: Group foods you commonly use in meals, such as pasta with sauces, rice with beans, or baking ingredients (flour, yeast, sugar).

Snacks & Quick Meals: Keep items like protein bars, trail mixes, and instant soups together for easy access to snacks or fast meals.

Cooking Essentials: Condiments, oils, herbs, and spices should be grouped for quick access during meal preparation.

By organizing according to usage, you simplify meal planning and make finding what you need when cooking easier.

Separating DIY from Store-Bought Items

If your storage includes both DIY-preserved and store-bought items, keep these separate. DIY-preserved foods may have different storage needs, expiration dates, and nutritional considerations. Grouping them will make it easier to monitor your homemade stock for signs of spoilage or when rotation is needed.

First In, First Out (FIFO)

Proper stock rotation is key to keeping your pantry organized and efficient. By rotating your stock regularly, you can ensure your food stays fresh and safe to eat while also reducing waste. The FIFO method, which uses the oldest items first, is a popular way to keep things in order. This section offers helpful tips and strategies for effectively rotating your pantry stock to always have a consistent inventory and avoid surprises.

Benefits

Prevents Waste: Regularly using older items before newer ones helps prevent food from expiring and going to waste.

Maintains Freshness: Ensures that your food is within its best quality and nutritional value period.

Improves Organization: This keeps your pantry organized and makes it easier to manage your inventory.

Cost-Effective: Reduces the need to discard expired food, saving you money in the long run.

Training and Involvement

Family Involvement: All household members are involved in the stock rotation process. Educate them on the importance of using older items first.

Consistent Practice: Make stock rotation a consistent practice. Regularly remind family members to follow the FIFO method.

Tips for Effective Stock Rotation

Easy Access: Design your pantry layout to facilitate access to older items. To keep smaller items organized, use bins or baskets.

Clear Containers: Clear containers are used for dry goods to easily see the contents and their quantities.

Shelving Systems: Consider using adjustable or pull-out shelving systems to make accessing items, especially those at the back, easier.

Label Shelves: Label shelves with the category of items stored there, making it easier to track where everything belongs.

Regular Updates: Update your inventory list regularly as you add or use items. This helps maintain accurate records and simplifies the rotation process.

Follow these steps and tips to keep your pantry organized and your food fresh. By rotating your stock regularly, you'll not only save money but also ensure that your food stays safe to eat:

Step-by-Step FIFO

Here is a simple step-by-step guide for using the FIFO method to manage your food storage:

Step 1: Label and Date

Purchase Date: Mark each item with the date of purchase using a permanent marker, label maker, or stickers. This helps identify the age of each item.

Expiration Date: Clearly label the expiration date on each item. If the date is not already printed on the packaging, write it yourself.

Visible Labels: Ensure labels are visible without having to move items around. Place labels on the front or top of containers.

Step 2: Organize by Date

Oldest in Front: Place older items at the front of shelves and newer items at the back. This makes it easy to grab the items that need to be used first.

Newest in Back: When adding new items to your pantry, move existing items forward and place new items behind them. This maintains the rotation system.

Step 3: Track Inventory

Inventory List: Keep an up-to-date inventory list that includes purchase dates and expiration dates. This helps you monitor what needs to be used soon.

Digital Tools: Consider using digital tools or apps to track your inventory and set reminders for items nearing their expiration dates.

Free Food Apps

Here are some free Apps you can consider to help with the management of your food stockpile:

***USDA FoodKeeper App*:** Developed by the USDA's Food Safety and Inspection Service, this app offers guidance on the safe handling, preparation, and storage of foods. It provides specific storage timelines for various products, helping you maximize freshness and reduce waste.

https://www.foodsafety.gov/keep-food-safe/foodkeeper-app

FEMA App: While primarily designed for disaster preparedness, the FEMA App includes features that can assist in managing emergency food supplies. It offers real-time weather and emergency alerts, information on nearby shelters, and resources for disaster recovery.

https://www.fema.gov/fact-sheet/use-fema-app-take-charge-your-disaster-recovery

Shop Simple App: Designed to help users manage grocery lists, track purchases, and streamline meal planning, making it a useful tool for everyday shopping. While it is primarily intended for organizing shopping trips, it can also be adapted for tracking food inventory, which is especially helpful for preppers or anyone managing a large stockpile of food.

https://www.myplate.gov/app/shopsimple

Wrapping it Up...

Organizing your pantry and stockpile is vital for a reliable and efficient food storage system. Using strategies like First In, First Out (FIFO), setting up the proper storage conditions, and picking suitable containers ensure your supplies stay fresh and easy to access. Plus, regularly tidying up, checking what you have, and restocking will help you adjust to changing needs, prevent food boredom, and make the most of what you've got. A well-managed pantry gives you peace of mind and flexibility, so you're always ready to handle whatever comes your way.

> **Key Points**
>
> **Optimize Storage Conditions:** It is important to keep your stockpile and pantry neat and organized to keep your food fresh and safe to eat.
> **Storage in Small Spaces:** Be creative and stay organized for small spaces.
> **Waterproofing Food Storage:** To prevent moisture-related spoilage, mold, and contamination.
> **Food Storage Containers:** Store your food correctly to keep it fresh and safe by choosing suitable food containers.
> **3-Tier Food Storage Method:** Store foods in Short (Tier 1), Intermediate (Tier 2), and Long-term (Tier 3) categories for easy access and maintenance.
> **FIFO Step-by-Step:** Follow the steps to implement the First-in, First-out method to organize and rotate your foods.

Online Resources

- Ready.gov: A U.S. government website that offers comprehensive guides on preparing for emergencies, including food and water storage. http://ready.gov

- Centers for Disease Control and Prevention (CDC) - The

CDC provides resources and guidelines on emergency preparedness, including food safety and public health concerns during disasters. https://emergency.cdc.gov/

- EatByDate: Provides information on food shelf life and tips on managing special dietary needs within a stockpile. https://eatbydate.com/

- The Academy of Nutrition and Dietetics (EatRight): Provides nutrition and diet advice, including detailed guides on calories, macronutrients, and portion control. https://www.eatright.org/

7

CALCULATING FOOD STORAGE

Salt has no expiration date and was once so valuable it was used as currency.

When planning for long-term food storage, ensuring you have enough food to meet your household's nutritional and caloric needs is essential. By this point in the book, you should have a solid grasp of nutrition, diet, food preservation, and how to manage your food supplies. You might even have started compiling your list of essential foods.

At this point, you might wonder how much food you should store. In this chapter, we will explore three methods for calculating food quantities and provide example calculations for each method to help clarify the process.

Key Components

Before we discuss the methods, let's examine the key components you'll need to calculate your food storage.

Household

The people in your household who will depend on that stockpile for meals. Identifying who's in your household helps you figure out how much and what kinds of food you need to have on hand to keep everyone satisfied.

Factors to Consider

Size and Composition: Adults, children, infants, and elderly members may have different caloric and nutritional needs.

Activity Levels: Physically active individuals may require more calories.

Special Dietary Needs: Consider allergies, medical conditions, or dietary preferences (e.g., vegetarian, gluten-free).

Essential Foods

These must-have foods are the backbone of a solid food storage strategy, ensuring your household gets the vital nutrients it needs while you rely on your stash. In the *Essential Foods* chapter, we discussed compiling a list of these foods and showed an example list.

Storage Period

Food storage usually falls into -term, medium-term, or long-term categories. This time frame helps you determine how much food you need and what types to choose, depending on how long they last. If you're looking at longer storage times, you'll want more durable, shelf-stable options.

Common Storage Periods

Short-Term: 1-3 months (e.g., for emergencies or seasonal shortages).

Medium-Term: 3-12 months (e.g., economic downturns, supply chain issues).

Long-Term: 1 year or more (e.g., off-grid living, large-scale disasters).

Food Group Ratios

It's all about ensuring your *Food Survival plan* includes a good mix of the five major food groups. Keeping the proper ratios helps you stay nutritionally balanced, avoid deficiencies, and give you the energy and variety you need to keep everyone in the household happy and healthy. Here is a good balanced ratio for long-term food storage:

Carbohydrates	30-40%
Proteins	15-25%
Fats & Oils	15-20%
Fruits and Vegetables	15-20%
Dairy	10-15%

Calculating food quantities based on these ratios ensures you get the right foods in each food group.

Servings Size and Calories per Serving

Serving sizes and calories per serving are essential for determining how much food to store long-term. This information helps you calculate food storage based on calories and your household's nutritional requirements.

Serving Size

A Serving Size is a specific amount or portion of food defined by nutrition guidelines, such as those from the USDA, to help you understand how much of a food item to consume. Serving Sizes and Calories per Serving are key for calculating long-term food storage quantities.

For example, one serving of uncooked rice is approximately 1 oz (equivalent to half a cup of cooked rice), and one serving of peanut butter is two tablespoons.

Calories per Serving Size

The Calories per Serving indicate the amount of energy provided by one serving of food. It helps in meeting daily caloric requirements. For our examples above, the caloric content per serving is:

Rice   102 calories/1 oz

Peanut Butter   95 calories/2 tbsp

It is worth noting that calorie counts and serving sizes can vary due to several factors. Different dietary guidelines, such as those from the USDA and other countries, may define serving sizes differently. Additionally, food preparation methods and variations in brands and types (like whole grain versus refined) can affect calorie content.

We have used the food serving and caloric data from the (USDA) website for our calculations.

Methods for Calculating Food Storage Quantities

We will examine three methods for calculating food storage quantities, each offering unique advantages depending on your goals, dietary preferences, and available resources. Two common approaches are the **Caloric Needs Method** and the **Servings-Based Method**. The **LDS Food Storage Calculator** is an online tool to determine bulk food quantities.

Example Calculations

To better understand how these methods work, we will step through each process using an example household for 3-month food storage. We will use the example essential foods list we put together in the *Nutrition and Diet* chapter for the *Caloric* and *Servings* methods. The *LDS* Calculator uses a predefined set of foods.

Household

Our example household will comprise the following two adults and two children for a food storage period of 90 days:

Man 32 years (Moderately Active)

Women 31 years (Pregnant)

Child 4 Years old (Preschooler)

Child 8 years old (School-aged)

Food Groups Ratios

We will use these recommended long-term food group ratios:

Carbohydrates	35%
Proteins	20%
Fats & Oils	15%
Fruits and Vegetables	15%
Dairy	15%

Caloric Needs Method

Our first method focuses on ensuring that each person in a household has enough calories to meet their daily energy needs over a set period. Food quantities are then calculated based on meeting those caloric requirements for each food group.

Pros

- Provides a precise estimate based on energy needs.
- Ensures balanced macronutrient intake (carbohydrates, proteins, and fats).
- Ideal for customizing storage for individual or family health requirements.

Cons

- Requires detailed food data, including caloric and macronutrient content for each item.
- Time-consuming without the help of spreadsheets or software.

Step 1: Calculate Daily Caloric Needs

Look to the *Caloric Needs* section in the *Nutrition and Diet* chapter to determine the average day caloric requirements. For our example household, we adjust for the key variables (in this case, the Moderately Active adult male and Pregnant adult female). This gives us these adjusted caloric needs:

Man 33 yrs (Moderately Active + 600):	3,200 calories/day
Women 31 yrs (Pregnant + 400):	2,500 calories/day
Child 4 yrs (Preschooler):	1,400 calories/day
Child 8 yrs (School-aged):	1,800 calories/day
Total	**8,900 calories/day**

Step 2: Multiply by Storage Period

We multiply the daily calories by the storage period (90 days) to get the total calories for each food group:

8,900 calories / day x 90 days = **801,000 calories**

Step 3: Total calories for each Food Group

We can now allocate calories to each food group using our adopted food group ratios. These are the calories the household needs to meet their energy requirements:

Carbohydrates 35%	= 280,350 calories
Proteins 20%	= 160,200 calories
Fats & Oils 15%	= 120,150 calories
Fruits and Vegetables 15%	= 120,150 calories
Dairy 15%	= 120,150 calories

| Total | = 801,000 calories |

Step 4: Assign Quantities to Essential Foods

Now, we assign quantities to our example essential foods until the total calories for each food group approximately match.

You can see the combined tabulated results of the *Caloric* and *Servings* methods later in this chapter.

Servings-Based Method

This method ensures a balanced diet by calculating the number of food servings from each major food group over a given period. You then allocate quantities to each food to match the totals for each food group.

Pros

- Easier to follow for beginners.
- Focuses on a variety of food types, ensuring balanced meals.
- Compatible with pre-packaged or unitized food storage plans.

Cons

- May overlook specific caloric requirements.
- Serving sizes may not reflect actual consumption habits or caloric needs.

Step 1: Determine Daily Servings

Follow nutritional guidelines for the number of servings for each food group. We can use this table with the recommended number of food servings (from the USDA's website) for all household members based on age and gender.

	Number of Servings					
	Grains (oz)	Protein (oz)	Fats & Oils (tsp)	Fruits (cups)	Vegetables (cups)	Dairy (cups)
Toddler (12-23 months)	1.75 to 3	2	1.5 to 2	0.5 to 1	0.67 to 1	1.67 to 2
Children (2 to 3 yrs)	3 to 5	2 to 4	3	1 to 1.5	1 to 1.5	2 to 2.5
Children (4 to 8 yrs)	4 to 6.5	3 to 5.5	4	1 to 2	1.5 to 2.5	2.5
Girls (9 to 13 yrs)	5 to 7	4 to 6	5	1.5 to 2	1.5 to 3	3
Girls (14 to 18 yrs)	6 to 8	5 to 6.5	5 to 6	1.5 to 2	2.5 to 3	3
Boys (9 to 13 yrs)	5 to 9	5 to 6.5	5 to 6	1.5 to 2	2 to 3.5	3
Boys (14 to 18 yrs)	6 to 10	5.5 to 7	6 to 7	2 to 2.5	2.5 to 4	3
Women (19 to 30 yrs)	6 to 8	5 to 6.5	5 to 6	1.5 to 2	2.5 to 3	3
Women (31 to 59 yrs)	5.5 to 7	5 to 6	6 to 7	1.5 to 2	2 to 3	3
Women (60+ yrs)	5 to 7	5 to 6	5	1.5 to 2	2 to 3	3
Men (19 to 30 yrs)	8 to 10	6.5 to 7	6 to 7	2 to 2.5	3 to 4	3
Men (31 to 59 yrs)	7.5 to 10	6 to 7	5 to 6	2 to 2.5	3 to 4	3
Men (60+ yrs)	6 to 9	5.5 to 6.5	5 to 6	2	2.5 to 3.5	3

Step 2: Total Servings for the Household

Add up all the daily servings for each member to get a total for the household for each food group.

Step 3: Multiply by Storage Period

Multiply the daily servings by storage period (90 days) to get the total servings for each food group. This table shows the daily servings for our household, and the total servings for each food group:

	Grains (oz)	Protein (oz)	Fats & Oils (tsp)	Fruits (cups)	Vegetables (cups)	Dairy (cups)
Men (31-59 yrs)	9	6.75	7	2.25	3.50	3
Women (31-59 yrs)	7	5.75	6	1.75	2.75	3
Children (4-8 yrs) x 2	10	8.50	8	3	4	5
Total Daily	26	21	21	7	10	11
Total 90 Days	2,340	1,890	1,890	630	923	990

Step 4: Assign Quantities to Essential Foods

Now, as we did with the *Caloric* method, we assign quantities to our example essential foods until the total servings for each food group approximately match.

Caloric and Servings Methods Calculation Results

Here are the results for the *Caloric* and *Servings* methods for our example household. The first column lists each food group's total required calories and servings (underlined). These amounts align with the total calculated quantities for the food groups.

Just a heads up, the table includes only the major food groups and not the taste and comfort foods we have included in the example essential foods. We'll tackle the quantities for those separately.

Comparing Results

Let's do a quick comparison of the results:

Grains and Fruit & Veg: The *Caloric* method includes more Carbs / Grains and Fruits & Vegetables because it focuses on meeting energy needs first, prioritizing calorie-dense grains and carbohydrate-rich produce to meet daily calorie requirements.

Protein and Fats & Oils: The *Servings* method has more Protein and twice the Fats & Oils because it aims to ensure a nutrient-dense, balanced diet that supports overall health, not just energy needs.

Dairy: Similar quantities for each method.

LDS Food Storage Calculator Method

The *LDS Calculator* is a handy tool created to support the preparedness goals of The Church of Jesus Christ of Latter-day Saints, which has been all about self-reliance since the 1800s. It's all about stocking up on essential staple foods like grains, legumes, fats, and other must-haves, so you're good to go for a year or more. The calculator keeps it straightforward, focusing on bulk storage instead of getting bogged down with calorie counting or servings.

Pros

- Fast and user-friendly.
- Provides a solid baseline for a one-year food supply.
- Offers flexibility to adjust quantities based on household size and preferences.

Cons

- Less customizable for unique dietary needs.
- Focuses on staple foods, which may require supplementation for nutritional completeness.
- Uses only fresh foods for the fruit and vegetable group

Step 1: Access the *LDS* calculator

Using the calculator is very straightforward. There are a few ways you can access it:

Online: The internet version seems to have been removed from the *LDS* website, but you can find a version here:.

Use The App: You can install the free Microsoft App on your PC:

Spreadsheet: Get a copy of the *LDS Calculator* in the free spreadsheet. See the *Essential Foods* chapter on downloading and copying the spreadsheet.

Step 2: Enter Household Information and Storage Period

Input the number of Adults (7 yrs and up) and Children (0 to 6 yrs) in your household.

The website version time frame is set for 12 months only. You can input your storage period (in months) for the App and spreadsheet.

Step 3: Get Food and Quantity recommendations

Based on average needs, the calculator estimates major food groups, such as grains, legumes, fats, sugars, dairy, and other essentials. It will also suggest quantities of each item, such as how many pounds of rice, beans, or sugar you need to store.

LDS Calculator Results

Here is the output from the *LDS Calculator* for our example household for 3 months. I've included the calculated equivalent servings to make it easier to compare with the other methods.

PREPPER'S FOOD SURVIVAL PLAN

	Servings	Food	Quantity
Grains / Carbs		Rice	38 lbs
		Pasta	19 lbs
		Oats	19 lbs
		Corn Meal	19 lbs
		Flour	19 lbs
		Wheat	113 lbs
	3,629		*224 lbs*
Proteins (Legumes)		Beans, dry	22.5 lbs
		Lima Beans	3 lbs
		Soy Beans	7.5 lbs
		Split Peas	3 lbs
		Lentils	3 lbs
		Dry Soup Mix	3 lbs
	454		*42 lbs*
Fats and Oils		Vegetable Oil	3 lbs
		Shortening	2 gal
		Mayonnaise	2 qts
		Salad Dressing	1 qts
	1,393	Peanut Butter	3 lbs
Fruits & Vegetables		Flavored Apples	30 lbs
		Applesauce	30 lbs
		Banana Chips	22.5 lbs
		Fruit Mixture	26 lbs
		Fruit Juices	30 lbs
			139 lbs
		Corn	22.5 lbs
		Peas	22.5 lbs
		Green Beans	22.5 lbs
		Carrots	22.5 lbs
		Potatoes	30 lbs
		Onions	4 lbs
		Tomatoes	15 lbs
	1,467		*139 lbs*
Sweeteners	*N/A*	Honey	2 lbs
		Sugar	30 lbs
		Brown Sugar	2 lbs
		Molasses	1 lbs
		Corn Syrup	2 lbs
		Jams	2 lbs
		Fruit drink powdered	5 lbs
		Flavored Gelatin	1 lbs
			45 lbs
Dairy		Dry Milk	45 lbs
		Evaporated Milk	9 cans
	800	Other	9 lbs
Other	*N/A*	Baking Powder	1 lbs
		Baking Soda	1 lbs
		Yeast	0.5 lbs
		Salt	4 lbs
		Vinegar	0.5 gal
		Water - Drinking	365 gal
		Bleach - Sanitation	26 gal
	7,743		

Analysis

Here is an assessment of the *LDS* outputs compared to accepted nutritional guidelines:

Grains: This is higher than accepted guidelines, with approximately 47% of the total for the major food groups. For long-term food storage, grains are recommended in the 30-40% range.

Protein: The Legumes group includes the protein requirement but only supplies 6% compared to the recommended 15-25%. No meat or fish is included in the protein foods.

Fruit: Includes a mix of fresh and preserved fruits.

Vegetables: Only specifies fresh vegetables.

Sweeteners: Sweeteners are not typically seen as a major food group; they are viewed as empty calories, providing energy without essential nutrients. Also, the output includes brown sugar, which is not a good option for long-term storage because of its moisture content.

Food Group Ratios: The food group ratios (excluding Sweeteners) are unbalanced, with higher Grains / Carbs and lower Protein:

Grains / Carbs	47%
Proteins	6%
Fats & Oils	18%
Fruits and Vegetables	19%
Dairy	10%

Comfort Foods: Some comfort foods, including jams and flavored gelatin, are in the sweeteners category.

Cooking Essentials: Baking soda/powder, yeast, and vinegar are used for baking.

Salt: Essential for flavoring and food preservation.

Water: Critical component, and 1 gallon per person per day is recommended for both drinking water and water for food preparation.

Bleach: The only non-food included in the output for general sanitation and disinfection.

Comparing The Three Methods Results

We can make a rough quantitative comparison between the three methods using equivalent total servings for each food group. It's not a perfect comparison, but it does give us a way to compare methods.

	Total Servings		
	Caloric	Servings	LDS Calculator
Grains / Carbs	2,730	2,340	3,629
Proteins	1,384	1,886	454
Fats and Oils	980	1,890	1,393
Fruits & Vegetables	2,120	1,550	1,467
Dairy	940	990	800
Total	8,154	8,656	7,743

The table below shows the major food group ratios for each method. The *Caloric* method ratios are as we adopted for the calculation based on calories, not servings. For the *Servings* method we used the nutritional recommended number of servings for the household for each food group.

	Food Group Ratios		
	Caloric	Servings	LDS Calculator
Grains / Carbs	35%	27%	47%
Proteins	20%	22%	6%
Fats & Oils	15%	22%	18%
Fruits & Vegetables	15%	18%	19%
Dairy	15%	11%	10%
Total	100%	100%	100%

Analysis

Grains / Carbs: The *LDS Calculator* loads up on grains, which at 47% is considered a little high for the long-term recommended range of 30-40%. The grains for the *Servings* method are just outside this recommended range.

Protein: The *LDS Calculator* only supplies approximately 6% of protein, lower than the recommended 15-25%. Legumes are used for protein; however, the content is pretty low at just 0.1 ounces for every ounce of legumes. The other methods include essential foods like meat and fish, which pack approximately three times the protein of legumes.

Food Group Ratios: The *Caloric* method ratios are within accepted ranges. In the *Servings* method, grains are light, and fats & oils are heavy. The *LDS Calculator* quantities are unbalanced; reducing grains and increasing protein would make the *LDS* quantities more aligned with accepted guidelines.

LDS Sweeteners: The *LDS* has its own Sweeteners category. Though not part of the major food group ratios, sweeteners help preserve and boost flavor and are versatile for cooking and baking. Quantities are quite high, increasing overall calories.

Summary of Key Differences

Now, let's summarize the main differences between the methods for various other measures.

	Caloric Method	Servings Method	LDS Calculator
Ease of Use	Requires detailed calculations for each individual's daily caloric & nutritional needs.	Focuses on servings per food group, simpler than calorie counting but less precise.	Very simple; bulk storage guidelines for long-term emergencies.
Focus	Meeting precise caloric needs, with emphasis on balancing nutrients.	Balancing daily servings from each food group to ensure a varied diet.	Bulk storage of staple foods (grains, legumes, fats) for long-term emergencies.
Variety	Encourages more variety to meet nutritional & caloric needs.	Provides variety, focusing on balanced servings from all food groups.	Limited variety, focusing on bulk storage of staples
Nutritional Balance	Ensures balanced nutrition through precise control of calories & nutrients.	Emphasizes serving sizes but may not ensure exact caloric or nutritional needs.	Less focus on balanced nutrition; emphasizes bulk calories.
Adaptability	Highly adaptable to dietary preferences; includes a variety of preserved foods	Moderately adaptable; focuses on balanced servings of preserved foods	Less adaptable to diverse tastes; limited preserved options
Sugars / Sweeteners	Moderate for energy & flavor	Moderate for energy & flavor	Higher for preservation, flavor, & calories
Grains	Typically a higher proportion than the *Servings* method but lower than the *LDS* Calculator.	Balanced servings of grains, typically less than *LDS* & *Calorie* methods.	47% of total storage (e.g., wheat, rice, oats).
Protein	Precise protein intake from a mix of sources (meat, legumes, etc.), ensuring 100% of required protein.	Ensures adequate servings of protein through various food groups (meat, legumes).	Primarily legumes providing only around only 6% of the recommended 15-25%.

> **Key Takeaway**
>
> The *Caloric Needs Method* provides the most precise control of daily caloric intake with a balanced diet but requires detailed planning and calculations. Good for smaller households
>
> The *Servings Based Method* focuses on variety and simplicity by ensuring balanced servings from different food groups. However, it may lack precision in calories and total protein intake. Also suitable for smaller households
>
> The *LDS Food Storage Calculator* is best for long-term bulk storage, focusing heavily on grains and sweeteners. It is simple but lacks precision in nutrient balance. Carbs / Grains are higher, and Protein is lower than recommended.

Taste and Comfort Foods

Taste and comfort foods, while not part of the major food groups and thus not included in the quantities calculated in the *Caloric* or *Servings* methods, are crucial for enhancing taste, mood, and morale.

The following table includes examples of these foods with quantities. Sugar, salt, and vinegar have been loaded up since they are used in DIY food preservation. For the other foods, remember that these amounts can vary based on personal preferences. For example, I suggest 2 cups of coffee daily for adults, but I usually drink about 5 cups myself!

Remember that the extra calories from these foods aren't counted in the *Caloric* or *Servings* methods, so it's something to monitor.

	Taste & Comfort Foods	Calories / Serving	Servings	Quantity	Notes
Herbs & Spices	Dried Herbs	2 / tsp	420	4 lbs	Based on regular use
	Spices	10 / tsp	420	4 lbs	Salt for both flavor and food preservation
	Salt	0	1500	14 lbs	
Condiments & Sauces	Vinegar	3 / tbsp	750	3 gal	Additional vinegar if used for food preservation.
	Soy & Hot Sauce, Ketchup	10 / tbsp	380	1.5 gal	
Comfort Foods	Chocolate[1]	160 / oz	180	17 lbs	Based on daily consumption
	Granola Bars	150 / bar	180	180 bars	
Beverages	Coffee (Ground)	2 / tbsp	360	22.5 lbs	Based on daily consumption. Consider a variety of powdered drinks for added hydration.
	Tea	0 / tea bag	180	180 bags	
	Powdered Drinks[1]	115 / tbsp	270	17 lbs	
	Fruit Juices[1]	130 / cup	175	11 gal	
Other Essentials	Baking Powder / Soda, Yeast	10 / tsp	210	2 lbs	Based on baking frequency
	Sugar[1]	16 / tsp	1500	14 lbs	Extra sugar for food preservation.
	Honey[1]	21 / tsp	400	0.5 gal	Very Long Shelf Life
	Vitamin Supplements	0			As required

Your Food Storage Calculations

Now that we have completed example calculations and compared results, let's examine the options for calculating your long-term food storage quantities.

For the *Caloric* and *Servings* method, you'll need servings and calorie information for each of your essential foods. Appendix A lists common preserved foods and calorie counts per serving to make things easier. If you can't find what you're looking for, visit the USDA MyPlate https://www.myplate.gov/website for more details.

For Options 1 & 2, add your own Taste and Comfort foods separately.

Option 1: Caloric and Servings Based Methods

These methods are good for calculating your food quantities, but they do require some number crunching. The good news is if you download the spreadsheet you will get the *Prepper's Food Survival Calculator* that will make things much easier. This tool incorporates dropdown lists and formulas, making everything much more manageable. If you're familiar with spreadsheets, this is the way to go. The spreadsheet will have step by step instructions on how to use the *calculator*.

If spreadsheets are not your friend, then Option 2 would be a better fit as it simplifies the process by using a amended *LDS Calculator* to estimate quantities.

Option 2: Amended LDS Calculator

The *LDS Calculator* is user-friendly but doesn't provide balanced results from the major food groups. It recommends fresh fruits and vegetables, leaving out preserved or long-lasting options.

The amended version now balances the food groups by including preserved foods like DIY canned, dehydrated, frozen, and freeze-dried items while excluding fresh produce. I've also reduced the amount of sweeteners by about 30%, making it more balanced.

For those who may be hesitant to use spreadsheets, this simplified approach means you can get results without having to use a spreadsheet.

While the amended version may not be as precise as the *Caloric* or *Servings* methods, it offers a good range and balance of foods from different groups. The quantities suggested by the *LDS Calculator* are typically considered conservative, so the estimates in the amended version are likely to be higher rather than lower, providing a more satisfying meal plan.

Here's how to use the Amended *LDS Calculator*:

Step 1: Input your Household and Storage Period

The *Amended LDS Calculator* is only available in the spreadsheet. As with the original, enter the number of adults and children and the storage period in months.

Step 2: Review Results

Rebalancing of the food groups will give you ratios within these recommended ranges:

Grains / Carbs	30-40%
Proteins	15-25%
Fats & Oils	15-20%
Fruits and Vegetables	15-20%
Dairy	10-15%

The Sweeteners category is lowered by approximately one third.

Step 3: Substitute Your Essential Foods

With the *LDS* output, you can substitute foods with similar ones from your essential foods list. For example, in the Protein group, you could swap frozen meat for your own frozen beef.

If you're not using the spreadsheet, you can use the fillable table below to finalize your own food quantities. The amended *LDS* quantities are calculated for two adults and two children over 3 months, so you need to adjust for your household and storage period. The added foods are underlined:

	Amended LDS Calculator		Your Essential Foods	
	Food	Quantity	Food	Quantity
Grains	Rice	98 lbs		
	Pasta	15 lbs		
	Flour	15 lbs		
	Oats	15 lbs		
	Corn meal	34 lbs		
	Wheat	19 lbs		
Legumes (Protein)	Tuna (3oz Can)	135 cans		
	Canned Beef (DIY)	180 jars		
	Freeze-Dried Beef	19 lbs		
	Frozen Meat	45 lbs		
	Soy Beans	30 lbs		
	Split Peas	23 lbs		
	Lentils	23 lbs		
Fats & Oils	Nuts & Seeds	11 lbs		
	Olive Oil	1 gal		
	Vegetable Oil	2 gal		
	Mayonnaise	2 qts		
	Peanut Butter	3 lbs		
Fruits	Canned Fruit (DIY)	90 jars		
	Dried Fruits (DIY)	15 lbs		
	Freeze-Dried Fruits	15 lbs		
	Frozen Fruits	30 lbs		
	Fruit Juices	11 gal		
Vegetables	Canned Veg (DIY)	105 jars		
	Dried Vegetables	11 lbs		
	Freeze-Dried Veg	11 lbs		
	Frozen Vegetables	30 lbs		
Dairy	Powdered Milk	50 lbs		
	Evaporated Milk	10 cans		
	Other Diary	10 lbs		
Sweeteners	Honey	1.5 lbs		
	Sugar	21 lbs		
	Molasses	1 lbs		
	Corn Syrup	1.5 lbs		
	Jams	1.5 lbs		
	Fruit drink powdered	3 lbs		
Cooking Essentials	Baking Powder	1 lbs		
	Baking Soda	1 lbs		
	Yeast	0.5 lbs		
	Salt	4 lbs		
	Vinegar	0.5 gal		
Water	Drinking Water	365 gal		
	Bleach	26 gal		

Wrapping it Up...

Whether you diligently calculated your stockpile from scratch or used the amended *LDS Calculator*, many factors can mess with the final amounts you'll need. Things like how big your servings are, the density of the food, changes in how many people are in your household, and everyone's unique dietary needs can all play a role. Plus, unexpected stuff like increased activity levels, changes in diet, or even food going bad can throw off your consumption rates, making it challenging to nail down exactly how much food you'll need.

Adding a little wiggle room to your calculations is a good idea to handle these uncertainties. Throwing in an extra 10-20% can act as a safety net, ensuring you've got enough food for those longer-than-expected emergencies or surprise situations. This little buffer gives you peace of mind, knowing your food storage plan is solid, flexible, and ready to keep your household going during tough times.

> **Key Points**
>
> **Example Household:** Illustrates differences in the three stockpile calculation methods.
> **Caloric Method:** Precise and suitable for small households, but requires detailed calculations.
> **Servings Based Method:** Good variety of foods and suitable for small households.
> **Original *LDS Calculator*:** Good for bulk quantities but lacks precision and has unbalanced food groups
> **Spreadsheet: Download to use the *LDS* and *Prepper's Food Survival* Calculators**
> **Amended *LDS Calculator*:** The revised calculator is on the spreadsheet. It substitutes fresh foods for preserved foods and rebalances the food groups to meet accepted guidelines.

Online Resources

These online resources offer useful information to help individuals and families:

- The Food Guys: *LDS Food Storage Calculator.* https://www.thefoodguys.com/foodcalc.html

- National Center for Home Food Preservation (USDA): Comprehensive guides on food preservation techniques, including considerations for different climates and environmental conditions. https://nchfp.uga.edu/

- USDA FoodData Central: Detailed nutritional information for various food items. https://fdc.nal.usda.gov/

- USDA MyPlate: Information on nutrition and healthy eating. Offers a variety of tools, guidelines, and resources to help individuals and families make healthier food choices. https://www.myplate.gov/

- Ready.gov: A U.S. government website that offers comprehensive guides on preparing for emergencies, including food and water storage. http://ready.gov

- EatByDate: Provides information on food shelf life and tips on managing special dietary needs within a stockpile. https://eatbydate.com/

- National Institutes of Health (NIH) - A resource for information on food, calories, and health. Includes tools for calorie counting, meal planning, and dietary guideline. https://www.nutrition.gov/

8

STEP-BY-STEP STOCKPILE BUILD

The largest private food stockpile ever built belonged to Howard Hughes, who stored over 2,000 cans of peas.

Now that we've explored the ins and outs of stockpiling food, it's time to pull everything together and create your stockpile. A well-stocked stockpile is crucial for ensuring you have a reliable supply of food and essentials, especially when things get unpredictable.

Here's a simple step-by-step guide to setting up a practical and efficient stockpile:

Step 1: Audit and Clean

Look at what food you currently have available:

Assessment: Take stock of what you currently have in your pantry. Make a list of all items, noting their quantities and expiration dates. This will help you identify items that need to be used soon, those that need to be restocked, and any duplicates.

Cleaning: Remove all items from your pantry and thoroughly clean the shelves, bins, and containers. Cleaning helps prevent pests and keeps your storage area hygienic.

Step 2: Assess Your Space

Identify any space limitations for your stockpile:

Evaluate Available Space: Identify all potential storage areas in your home, including kitchen cabinets, closets, under-bed spaces, and unused nooks.

Be creative: As we discussed earlier in this chapter, if you're in an apartment, make the most of your space by getting creative with your storage options.

Set a Budget: Determine how much you will spend building your pantry and stockpile. This will help guide your purchasing decisions.

Step 3: Your Food Sources

In the *Food Sources* chapter, you have identified your food sources, which could be from:

Fresh Food: Great for nutrients but doesn't last long.

Canned Foods: Convenient and long-lasting, no need for refrigeration.

Dry Foods: Grains, legumes, and more with a long shelf life.

Protein Bars and Drinks: Portable, easily stored sources of protein.

Meals Ready to Eat (MREs): Easy to store and prepare for the long term.

Store-bought Long-Life Foods: These foods are made to last long, making them convenient for preppers who want easy-to-store, ready-to-eat options.

DIY Preserved Food: Canned, Dehydrated, and Freeze-Dried items keep well and keep their nutrition.

Step 4: Your DIY Preserved Food

In the *Essential Foods* chapter, you listed the foods you want to preserve yourself. The choice will depend on factors such as fresh food sources, shelf life, storage space, and tools.

Step 5: Essential Foods

In the same chapter, you put together a list of your essential foods, which will form the foundation of your stockpile. This list features healthy options from all the major food groups that fit your household's diet and tastes. Plus, you threw in some taste and comfort foods to keep things tasty and boost everyone's mood.

Step 6: Stockpile Quantities

In the *Calculating Food Storage* chapter, you calculated quantities for your essential foods using one these options:

Option 1: Caloric and Servings-Based Methods: Follow the steps for the example household using your own household, storage period, and essential foods.

Option 2: Amended LDS Calculator —This is a simplified method that uses an amended *LDS* Calculator to estimate food quantities.

For each option, you will need to add your Taste and Comfort foods separately, which are based on your household's personal preferences.

Step 7: Stockpile and Pantry

In the *Your Stockpile and Pantry* chapter, you can:

Optimize your storage: Temperature control, low humidity, routine cleaning, etc., to ensure your foods stay in good shape.

Food Containers: Select the containers that best suit your essential foods, such as Mason Jars, Food-Grade buckets, Mylar bags, and Airtight containers.

Label Everything: Make sure to mark your containers' expiration dates and what's inside. This little step will help you stay organized and prevent any food waste.

Implement a Food Storage System: Use the 3-tier method: T1—short-term, T2—medium-term, and T3—long-term.

Use the FIFO Method: Follow the steps in the Your Stock & Pantry chapter to implement the First-in, First-out stock rotation method.

Step 8: Begin Small

Starting small is a great way to build your stockpile without feeling overwhelmed. Just think of it as a little project you can enjoy over time:

Begin with Weekly Additions: When you hit the grocery store, grab a few extra non-perishable items each week. It could be anything from canned beans to pasta or rice—whatever you know you'll use.

Buy in Bulk: If you can find a good deal on staples, go for it. It will save you money in the long run and mean you won't have to worry about running out of essentials anytime soon. Just remember to store everything correctly so it lasts.

Step 9: Stockpile on a Budget

Build your stockpile on a budget with planning, smart shopping, and creativity:

Plan and Prioritize

- Identify Essentials: Focus on staple foods that provide essential nutrients (grains, proteins, canned goods).

- Create a List: Organize by food type to avoid impulse buys and stay focused.

Set a Budget

- Monthly Allocation: Decide on a monthly stockpile budget from your grocery funds.

- Track Spending: Use a spreadsheet or app to stay on budget and adjust as needed.

Repurpose and Recycle

- Storage Solutions: Use glass jars, large containers, and repurposed furniture for food storage.
- Recycled Containers: Empty food containers (yogurt tubs, coffee cans) can store bulk items.

Smart Shopping Strategies

- Buy in Bulk: Save by purchasing rice, beans, pasta, and oats in large quantities.
- Sales & Coupons: Shop sales, use coupons, and buy store brands to cut costs.
- Seasonal Produce: Buy in-season fruits and veggies, then can, freeze, or dehydrate.

Stretching Your Budget

- Cook from Scratch: Homemade meals are cheaper; freeze leftovers and focus on essential ingredients.
- Reduce Waste: Use leftovers in new meals; compost scraps to enrich your garden soil.
- Grow Your Own Food: Use small spaces for container gardening and preserve your harvest.

Join a Community

- Community Gardens: Grow and share produce with others.
- Food Co-ops: Access discounted groceries and bulk buys as a member.

Step 10: Regularly Monitor and Update

Go through your pantry once a month to check for expiration dates and spoilage and to update your inventory.

Restock as Needed: As you use items, replace them to maintain your stockpile levels.

Adjust Based on Consumption: Track what you and your family use most often and adjust your stockpile accordingly.

Digital Inventory: Consider using an App or spreadsheet to manage food.

Wrapping it Up...

Building a well-organized and sustainable stockpile is important for being prepared and self-sufficient in the long run. Following these steps, you've set a solid foundation by starting with a clean-up and audit and creating a dedicated storage space. Each step, from picking your food sources to figuring out how much to stock, helps ensure your supplies are diverse and tailored to your household's needs.

Remember, minor adjustments can lead to significant changes, so take your time and tweak things. Keep an eye on your supplies to make sure everything stays fresh. This approach involves collecting supplies and building a flexible system that adapts to you.

> **Key Points**
>
> **Step-by-Step Stockpile Build:** Follow the steps to build your own stockpile.
> **Start Small:** Slowly build up your stockpile.
> **Stockpile on a Budget:** Create solid food storage without spending a fortune.

Online Resources

- Ready.gov: A U.S. government website that offers comprehensive guides on preparing for emergencies, including food and water storage. http://ready.gov

- USDA FoodData Central: Detailed nutritional information for various food items. https://fdc.nal.usda.gov/

- USDA MyPlate: Information on nutrition and healthy eating. Offers a variety of tools, guidelines, and resources to help individuals and families make healthier food choices.

- National Institutes of Health (NIH) - A resource for information on food, calories, and health. Includes tools for calorie counting, meal planning, and dietary guidelines. https://www.myplate.gov/

- Centers for Disease Control and Prevention (CDC) - The CDC provides resources and guidelines on emergency preparedness, including food safety and public health concerns during disasters. https://emergency.cdc.gov/

- Federal Emergency Management Agency (FEMA) - FEMA offers a range of resources on disaster preparedness, including detailed checklists for building emergency kits and ensuring food safety during power outages.

https://www.fema.gov/emergency-managers/individuals-communities/preparedness-activities-research-webinars

- EatByDate: Provides information on food shelf life and tips on managing special dietary needs within a stockpile. https://eatbydate.com/

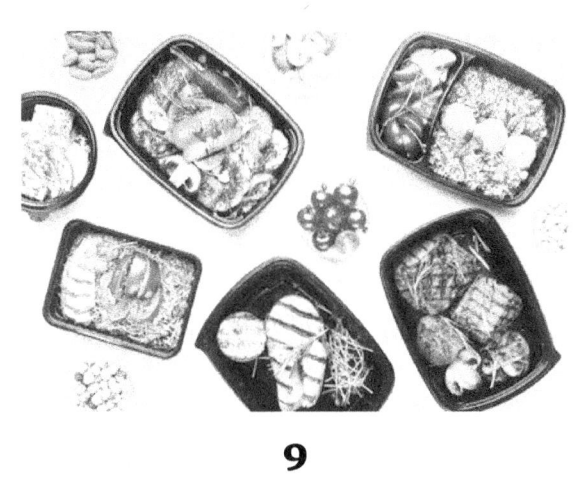

9

MEAL PLANNING

The phrase "square meal" originated from the practice of serving meals on square wooden plates aboard ships.

Planning meals is a crucial part of a successful *Food Survival Plan*. As previously discussed, having a solid food storage system involves knowing how to preserve food, including nutrient-packed superfoods, meeting calorie requirements, and using a strategic 3-Tier storage system. In this chapter, we'll combine all these factors to make meal plans that provide balanced nutrition and a range of options and make the most of your stored foods.

Why Meal Planning is Crucial

Meal planning is essential for anyone managing a well-stocked pantry to support their family, especially during emergencies. Here's why:

Nutritional Balance: Planning ensures balanced meals with essential nutrients, mainly when relying on preserved foods.

Variety & Enjoyment: Meal plans prevent fatigue by adding variety and keeping meals enjoyable over time.

Efficient Storage Use: Planning helps you use stored foods wisely, minimizing waste and preventing items from expiring.

Cost-Effective: Meal planning supports budgeting by enabling bulk buying, reducing waste, and avoiding last-minute purchases.

Reduces Stress: Knowing what to cook daily relieves decision-making pressure, which is particularly useful in emergencies.

Key Concepts

Maintaining a nutritious, well-rounded diet is crucial for health and energy, especially during uncertain times. Key concepts include:

Preservation Methods: Canning, freezing, dehydrating, and fermenting offer various options for keeping food fresh.

Nutrition Awareness: Understanding food contents supports both physical and mental well-being.

Superfoods: Including nutrient-dense foods helps cover essential nutrients during long-term storage.

Calories: Knowing each family member's caloric needs helps create energy-sustaining meal plans.

3-Tier Food Storage System: This system divides storage into short-, medium-, and long-term supplies, supporting smooth stock rotation.

Essential Foods: These items, tailored to your needs, form the base for long-term meal planning.

Meal Planning Goals

Effective meal planning helps optimize nutrition, extend food supplies, and simplify cooking:

Food Security: Use the 3-Tier Storage System—short-term perishables, medium-term canned goods, and long-term staples.

Balanced Nutrition: Include carbs, proteins, fats, preserved fruits, veggies, and superfoods.

Caloric Needs: Meet each person's daily caloric requirements.

Variety & Preferences: Rotate foods, add family favorites, and use themes like Meatless Monday.

Meal Prep: Batch-cook on lighter days and prep ingredients in advance for easy assembly.

Rotate Stock: Follow the FIFO method to reduce waste and label items for easy rotation.

Utilize Leftovers: Repurpose leftovers creatively for meal variety.

Efficiency: Focus on easy-to-prepare meals, one-pot dishes, and quick-cook items.

Emergency Preparedness: Keep high-calorie foods, hydration solutions, and ready-to-eat meals on hand.

Review & Adjust: Update plans seasonally and consider family feedback.

> ## Calorie Counting
>
> Calories are essential for meal planning and overall health, providing the energy your body needs. Instead of obsessively counting calories, a more effective approach is to regularly monitor your weight and adjust your carbohydrate intake as necessary. By focusing on balanced meals with the right portions of proteins, fats, and carbs, you can maintain your energy and health without the stress of constant tracking.

Avoiding Palate Fatigue

Eating the same foods all the time can lead to palate fatigue, dulling taste, and reduced appetite—an issue when relying on stockpiled foods. To prevent this, focus on variety to keep meals enjoyable and ensure balanced nutrition.

Balanced Pantry

Diversity: Stock a variety of proteins, grains, legumes, fruits, and vegetables to keep meals interesting (e.g., canned fish, dried beans, whole grains).

Fill Nutritional Gaps: Include powdered milk for calcium or canned fish for omega-3s to ensure a well-rounded diet.

Baking with Grains and Flour

Flexible and Nutritious: Flour is a staple for diverse recipes—bread, pasta, and pancakes—offering variety and better nutritional control with whole-grain or enriched options.

Cost-Effective: Baking from bulk flour saves money compared to pre-made goods.

Efficient Meal Prep: Make ahead items like bread or muffins to simplify meal planning and reduce prep time.

Comfort and Tradition: Homemade baked goods add warmth and familiarity to meals, providing comfort in challenging times.

Maintaining variety in your stockpile helps avoid palate fatigue, keeps nutrition balanced, and makes meals satisfying and enjoyable.

Snacks

Healthy snacks help maintain energy, stabilize blood sugar, and keep you from overeating at meals. A mix of protein, fats, and carbs in snacks can keep you satisfied, focused, and nourished, especially when fresh food is limited. Here are some easy, nutritious options:

Trail Mix: Combine dried fruits, nuts, and seeds.

Jerky: Beef, turkey, or plant-based varieties.

Canned Tuna or Salmon: Pair with crackers for a quick snack.

Dried Fruit: Options like apples, apricots, raisins, or berries.

Nut Butter: Try peanut or almond butter with rice cakes.

Granola Bars: Store-bought or homemade with oats, nuts, and dried fruit.

Seed Crackers: Flaxseed or chia-based.

Popcorn: Lightly salted or seasoned whole-grain option.

Protein Bars: High-protein options fortified with vitamins.

Drinks and Smoothies

Drinks and smoothies are convenient, nutrient-dense additions to your meal plan. They're flexible and perfect for using pantry staples when fresh produce isn't available. Here are some ideas:

Fruit and Nut Butter Smoothie: Canned peaches or pineapple, almond butter, powdered milk, ice, or water.

Protein-Packed Shake: Canned/powdered milk, protein powder, peanut butter, cacao powder.

Berry Blast Smoothie: Freeze-dried berries, shelf-stable yogurt, honey or agave, water or milk.

Electrolyte Drink: Coconut water, a pinch of salt, bottled lemon juice, honey.

Chocolate Banana Smoothie: Canned/powdered milk, cocoa powder, freeze-dried bananas, ice or water.

Boosters for Nutritional Value

Add superfoods to enhance the nutrition of your drinks:

Chia Seeds: Adds fiber and omega-3s.

Spirulina: Provides protein and antioxidants.

Powdered Greens: Adds nutrients without strong flavors.

Ground Flaxseeds: Adds fiber and a nutty flavor.

These versatile snack and drink options can help keep you nourished and energized, even with limited fresh ingredients.

Adjusting for Seasonal Changes

Adapting meals to the seasons helps ensure balanced nutrition, cost savings, and access to fresh ingredients, especially in emergencies. Here are key tips for seasonal meal planning:

Seasonal Produce: Use locally available fruits and veggies to maximize nutrients and save money.

Preservation Techniques: Preserve seasonal produce for use during off-seasons.

Menu Flexibility: Keep menus adaptable based on what's in season.

Nutritional Balance: Vary food choices with the seasons to maintain essential nutrients.

Storage Adjustments: Modify storage based on seasonal temperature and humidity to protect food quality.

Cooking Methods: Opt for lighter cooking in summer and heartier meals in winter.

Budget-Friendly: Take advantage of seasonal discounts to stretch your budget.

Budgeting for Meal Planning

Meal planning on a budget helps control costs while keeping meals nutritious and enjoyable. Here's how:

Set a Budget: Determine a weekly or monthly food budget.

Plan Around Sales: Design meals based on grocery store discounts.

Buy in Bulk: Save on staples like grains, beans, and canned goods.

Use Seasonal Produce: Seasonal fruits and veggies are often cheaper and fresher.

Limit Processed Foods: Avoid pricey pre-packaged foods by cooking at home.

Affordable Proteins: Choose budget-friendly options like beans, lentils, eggs, and canned fish.

Reduce Food Waste: Plan to use leftovers, maximizing each purchase.

By aligning meal plans with the seasons and budgeting effectively, you can create a resilient, cost-effective approach to meal planning that keeps your family well-fed year-round.

Meal Plans

Meal plans support long-term food security while providing a nutritious and diverse diet. They're helpful even outside of emergencies. You can keep everything fresh and avoid waste by including stockpiled foods in your meals. Plus, sticking to meal plans helps you maintain a balanced diet and manage your supplies, so you won't have to scramble to restock when running low.

7-Day Meal Plan

A seven-day meal plan includes breakfast, lunch, dinner, and snacks, focusing on proteins, carbs, and healthy fats. Emphasizing fresh ingredients and seasonal produce, it features quick meals for busy days and more elaborate options when you have time to cook. This plan simplifies grocery shopping and meal prep and helps you enjoy a healthy and satisfying diet all week.

Here is a simple guide to creating your 7-day meal plan:

7-Day Meal Plan Guide

Plan for three main meals (breakfast, lunch, dinner) and one daily snack.

Assess Nutritional Needs

- Determine the caloric and nutritional requirements for each family member.
- Ensure each meal balances proteins, carbohydrates, fats, vitamins, and minerals.

Inventory Check

- Review your pantry, fridge, and freezer to see what ingredients you already have.
- Note any items that need to be used soon to prevent waste.

Batch Cook

- Identify meals that can be prepped or batch-cooked in advance, making busy days easier.

Utilize Food Tiers

- Incorporate foods from the three tiers (T1: short-term, T2: intermediate-term, T3: long-term) to ensure a balanced use of your food supplies.
- Use fresh and perishable items (T1) early in the week and rely on preserved items (T2, T3) towards the end of the week.

Choose Diverse Meals

- Select a variety of recipes that incorporate different food groups and preservation methods (fresh, frozen, canned, dried).
- Consider themed days (e.g., Meatless Monday, Taco Tuesday) to add variety and structure.

Leftovers

- Plan for leftovers in subsequent meals, reducing waste and saving time.

Plan for Flexibility

- Include a few meals that are easy to adjust or substitute

if plans change.

- Have backup options like ready-made or quick-prep meals for busy days.

Prepare a Shopping List

- Create a detailed grocery list based on your meal plan to ensure you have all the necessary ingredients.

- For efficient shopping, group items by category (produce, dairy, pantry staples).

Here's an example 7-day meal plan that includes a mix of short-term (T1), intermediate-term (T2), and long-term (T3) food storage items. It offers a range of meals to keep things exciting and nutritious without getting bored with the menu.

	Breakfast	Lunch	Dinner	Snacks
Monday	Yogurt (perishable), fresh fruit (T1)	Sandwich: deli meat (T1), cheese (T2), bread (T3)	Grilled chicken (T1), frozen vegetables (T2), rice (T3)	Fresh fruit (T1), granola bars (T3)
Tuesday	Milk (perishable), cereal (T3), fresh berries (T1)	Salad: lettuce (T1), frozen corn (T2), canned beans (T2), vinaigrette (T3)	Frozen fish (T1), mashed potatoes (T3), frozen peas (T2)	Crackers (T3), cheese slices (T2)
Wednesday	Hard-boiled eggs (T1), bread (T3), butter (T3)	Canned tuna salad (T2), crackers (T3), pickles (T2)	Beef stew (T2, frozen if thawed), canned carrots (T2)	Nuts (T2), dried fruit (T2)
Thursday	Peanut butter (T3), bread (T3), apples (T1)	Lentil soup (T2, shelf-stable), whole wheat bread (T3)	Canned chicken (T2), canned green beans (T2), rice (T3)	Canned fruit (T2), trail mix (T3)
Friday	Instant oatmeal (T3) with dried fruit (T2)	Canned chili (T2), tortilla chips (T3)	Freeze-dried meal (T3), canned peas (T2)	Jerky (T2), energy bars (T3)
Saturday	Granola bars (T3), shelf-stable milk (T3)	Canned beans (T2), rice (T3), salsa (T2)	Shelf-stable pasta salad (T3), canned tuna (T2), olives (T2)	Nut butter packets (T3), crackers (T3)
Sunday	Shelf-stable protein shake (T3)	Peanut butter (T3), crackers (T3), canned fruit (T2)	Freeze-dried curry (T3), rice (T3), canned spinach (T2)	Cereal (T3), dried fruit (T2)

Create your 7-day meal plan by filling in the table or using the template in the free spreadsheet:

	Breakfast	Lunch	Dinner	Snacks
Monday				
Tuesday				
Wednesday				
Thursday				
Friday				
Saturday				
Sunday				

30-Day Meal Plan

A 30-day meal plan is about long-term sustainability and preparedness. Unlike a 7-day plan, which relies on fresh T1 foods, this plan focuses more on T2 preserved foods like canned and frozen items and T3 long-term staples such as rice, flour, and freeze-dried meals.

Incorporating these foods will reduce dependence on frequent shopping while maintaining a balanced and varied diet.

Making the Most of Your Preserved Foods

Using your preserved foods creatively can add flavor and variety to your meals while reducing waste. Here's how to get the most out of your pantry staples:

Canned Veggies and Soups: Add canned tomatoes, beans, or veggies to soups, stews, or casseroles for a quick, hearty meal.

Dried Fruits: Mix dried fruits into oatmeal, yogurt, baked goods, or rehydrate for sauces and salads.

Fermented Foods: Add sauerkraut or kimchi to sandwiches as sides, or stir into stir-fries for a flavor boost.

Elevating Everyday Meals

- Pickles and Relishes: Add crunch to sandwiches, burgers, and potato salads.
- Herbs and Seasonings: Use dried herbs on meats, pasta, and roasted veggies for added depth.
- Jams and Preserves: Swirl into yogurt, use in marinades, or add as pastry fillings.

Quick and Easy Meals

- Instant Soups and Stews: Combine canned veggies, beans, and broth for a fast, hearty soup.
- Pasta and Rice Dishes: Mix pasta or rice with preserved veggies, pickles, or sauces for a speedy, satisfying dish.
- Snack Boards: Create snack boards with preserved fruits, pickles, cured meats, and cheeses.

Culinary Adventures

- Global Inspirations: For international flair, try preserved lemons in Moroccan dishes, pickled ginger with sushi, or dried chilies in salsas.

- Infused Oils and Vinegar: Preserved herbs or garlic can be used to make flavorful oils and vinegars for dressings and marinades.

Reducing Waste and Maximizing Value

- First In, First Out: Use older preserves to keep pantry items fresh.

- Repurposing Leftovers: Get creative with leftovers, such as adding extra pickles to salads or turning fruit preserves into glazes.

By incorporating preserved foods into your meals, you can make cooking easier, prevent waste, and enjoy the results of your preservation efforts every day. Happy cooking!

Emergency Meal Planning

A solid emergency meal plan ensures survival and comfort during crises in an unpredictable world. Here's a quick guide that emphasizes the 3-tier food storage method.

Key Principles

Scenario Planning: Plan for emergencies, from short power outages to extended disruptions.

Balanced Nutrition: Maintain carbs, proteins, fats, vitamins, and minerals.

Ease of Prep: Choose foods needing minimal prep, considering limited water, fuel, or power.

Comfort Foods: Familiar items boost morale.

Emergency Meal Kit: Assemble a kit with non-perishable essentials for quick access.

Scenario Planning for Common Emergencies

Natural Disasters: Earthquake-proof storage, waterproof containers, and evacuation-ready kits.

Power Outages: Use perishables first, stock shelf-stable foods, and invest in alternative power for more extended outages.

Water Supply Issues: Store bottled water, use purifiers, and opt for foods requiring little water.

Economic Challenges: Stock bulk staples, grow food, and consider barter options.

Pandemic: Minimize trips with a well-stocked pantry; include immune-boosting foods.

Civil Unrest: Maintain a low profile with secure, discreet food storage.

Nuclear/Chemical Threats: Stock sealed foods in safe areas; have portable, uncontaminated supplies.

Loss of Shelter: Keep grab-and-go food bags and portable kits.

Terrorist Attacks: Maintain food supplies at home and work with ready-to-eat meals.

Personal Emergencies: For job loss or medical needs, stock budget-friendly, easy-to-prepare, nutrient-dense foods.

Preparing for various scenarios will ensure a reliable food supply through any crisis.

Example Emergency Meal Plan

In emergencies, having a detailed meal plan tailored to the specific scenario can make a significant difference in ensuring you and your family's well-being. Here is an example 7-day Meal Plan for a power outage.

Scenario: Power Outage

Key Considerations:

- Days 1-2: Use perishable foods and thawed frozen items.
- Days 3-7: Focus on shelf-stable and no-cook meals.
- Ensure you have plenty of potable water for drinking and food preparation.

If you can produce your electricity independently, you won't be as impacted by power outages. Having your own renewable energy system is a great way to be self-reliant. If you are looking for off-grid power supply options, then consider another book in the *Off The Grid* series called *Prepper's Food Survival Plan*. It will help you set up your renewable energy source.

https://mybook.to/rcSZq6y

Emergency Meal Kit

A ready-to-go emergency meal kit stocked with non-perishable foods and essential supplies can help nourish your household during short-term food shortages. Here's how to create one:

Step 1: Determine Duration and Size

Decide on Coverage: Plan for 3, 7, or 14 days based on your household size.

Calculate Needs: Estimate daily caloric requirements (2,000–2,500 calories per adult), considering any special dietary needs.

Step 2: Select Food Items

Non-Perishables:

- Canned Goods: Soups, veggies, meats, and fruits.
- Dry Goods: Rice, pasta, instant potatoes, and oatmeal.
- Protein: Peanut butter, jerky, canned beans, and fish.
- Comfort Foods: Crackers, chocolate, coffee, tea.

Ready-to-Eat Meals: Include MREs or freeze-dried meals.

Snacks and Hydration: Dried fruits, energy bars, nuts, bottled water (1 gallon/person/day), and water purification options.

Supplements: Multivitamins and dietary supplements.

Step 3: Essential Tools and Equipment

Cooking & Eating Supplies: Manual can opener, utensils, lightweight pots, disposable plates.

Food Storage: Resealable bags, airtight containers, and trash bags.

Water Storage & Purification: Collapsible containers and purification tablets.

Step 4: Organize and Pack the Kit

Categorize: Group items by meal (breakfast, lunch, dinner, snacks) and label with contents and expiration dates.

Container: Use a waterproof bin or backpack with frequently used items on top.

Meal Plan: Include a basic meal schedule to avoid monotony.

Step 5: Emergency Cooking Methods

Portable Stove: Include a camping stove with fuel.

Fire Starting: Waterproof matches, lighters, and fire starters.

Step 6: Add Extra Essentials

First Aid Kit: Bandages, antiseptics, medications.

Hygiene Supplies: Towelettes, hand sanitizer, biodegradable soap.

Miscellaneous: Multi-tool, flashlight, emergency blanket.

Step 7: Store and Maintain the Kit

Location: Store in a cool, dry place near an exit.

Regular Rotation: Check every 6 months to replace items near expiration.

Updates: Adjust based on household changes or dietary needs.

Following these steps, you'll create an emergency meal kit that includes everything needed for food security, cooking, and basic survival during challenging times.

Here's an example Emergency Meal Kit for two adults and two children for 3 days:

PREPPER'S FOOD SURVIVAL PLAN

	Item	Quantity	Purpose
Staples	Instant Rice	1 lb	Quick energy source, easy to prepare
	Instant Oatmeal	1 box	Breakfast, requires only hot water
	Pasta	1 lb	Versatile meal base, easy to cook
	Canned Beans	3 cans	Protein source, ready-to-eat
Proteins	Canned Tuna/Chicken	4 cans	Protein source, ready-to-eat
	Peanut Butter	1 small jar	Protein and fat, versatile spread
	Protein Bars	8 bars	Portable snack, protein and energy
Fruits and Vegetables	Canned Vegetables	4 cans	Nutrient source, ready-to-eat or heat
	Canned Fruit	4 cans	Sweet option, vitamins and energy
	Dried Fruit	0.5 lb	Long shelf life, vitamin-rich
Dairy	Shelf-Stable Milk	2 cartons	Source of calcium and protein
	Shelf-Stable Cheese	2 packages	Snack or meal, protein source
Fats and Oils	Cooking Oil	1 small bottle	For cooking and adding calories
	Shelf-Stable Butter	1 small jar	Cooking or spreading
Condiments and Spices	Salt	1 container	Enhances flavor
	Pepper	1 container	Enhances flavor
	Hot Sauce	1 small bottle	Adds flavor and variety
	Sugar Packets	10 packets	For sweetening drinks or meals
Beverages	Instant Coffee / Tea	6 packets	Provides caffeine and comfort
	Electrolyte Drink Mix	6 packets	Replenishes electrolytes
Snacks	Crackers	1 box	Pairs with peanut butter or cheese
	Trail Mix	0.5 lb	Energy snack, nuts and dried fruit
Miscellaneous	Multivitamins	1 bottle	Ensures essential nutrients are met
	Water	12 bottles	For drinking and meal preparation
	Water Purification Tablets	1 Packet	For safe drinking water
	Manual Can Opener	1	Essential tool
	First Aid Kit	1	Basic Kit, bandages, antiseptics
	Flashlight	1	With extra batteries
Emergency Cooking	Portable Stove	1	For cooking without electricity
	Fuel Canisters (for stove)	4	Provides fuel for cooking stove
	Matches/Lighter	1 pack	For lighting stove or starting a fire
	Mess Kit (pot, pan, utensils)	1 set	For cooking and serving meals
	Aluminum Foil	1 roll	For cooking, wrapping, or insulating

Now put your own Emergency Meal Kit together by filling in the table or using the template in the spreadsheet:

Item	Quantity	Purpose
Staples		
Proteins		
Fruits and Vegetables		
Dairy		
Fats and Oils		
Condiments and Spices		
Beverages		
Snacks		
Miscellaneous		
Emergency Cooking		

Water Usage

During emergencies, it's important to be mindful of how much clean water you use when cooking. Proper water management can help prevent contamination, save resources, and keep everyone healthy. Whether you're rehydrating food, cooking, or staying clean, using water wisely is key to successful emergency meal prep.

Key Considerations

Clean Water Sources: Ensure access to clean, potable water to prevent contamination and waterborne illnesses.

Conservation Techniques: Use water sparingly by reusing it safely, such as washing produce before boiling.

Efficient Cooking Methods: Opt for cooking methods that require less water, such as steaming or pressure cooking.

Food Selection: Choose foods that require minimal water for preparation, like pre-cooked or dehydrated options.

Hygiene Maintenance: Prioritize water for essential hygiene practices, including hand washing and sanitizing cooking utensils.

Water Purification: Implement methods for purifying available water, such as boiling, filtering, or using purification tablets.

Storage Solutions: Store water in clean, covered containers to keep it safe and readily accessible for food preparation and drinking.

Fuel and Cooking Resources

Having dependable fuel and cooking supplies for safe and healthy meals during emergencies is essential. Your fuel and cooking techniques can make a difference in how well you can cook and stay safe in a crisis. Here are some critical things to keep in mind when handling your fuel and cooking resources during emergencies:

Foods: Focus on ready-to-eat meals, dehydrated foods that require only soaking, and meals that can be prepared with alternative cooking methods (e.g., solar ovens, portable stoves).

Alternative Fuel Sources: Identify and stockpile alternative fuels such as propane, butane, kerosene, wood, or charcoal when electricity or gas lines are disrupted.

Portable Stoves: Invest in portable stoves or camping cookers that are easy to transport and operate on various fuel types.

Fuel Efficiency: Use fuel-efficient cooking methods, such as pressure cooking, to minimize fuel consumption and maximize resource longevity.

Safety Precautions: Ensure proper ventilation when using fuels that produce smoke or fumes, and follow safety guidelines to prevent fires and carbon monoxide poisoning.

Multi-Use Equipment: Choose versatile cooking equipment that can perform multiple functions (e.g., boiling, frying, baking) to reduce the need for multiple devices.

Fuel Storage: Store fuels safely in labeled, approved containers, away from living areas and potential ignition sources.

Matches and Lighters: Keep matches and lighters in an easily accessible location.

Contingency Planning: Plan for fuel shortages by having a backup plan, such as cold meal options or no-cook food items, to ensure food security even without fuel.

Meal Plans Regular Review

Regularly reviewing your meal plans is essential to ensure that your emergency preparedness remains effective and up-to-date. By keeping your meal plans current, you can be confident that, in an emergency, you will have the right foods on hand to sustain your household both physically and emotionally.

Weekly Checks: Conduct weekly checks of your meal plan and inventory. Adjust quantities and items based on what has been consumed and what needs replenishing.

Monthly Audits: Perform a more detailed monthly audit to check expiration dates, assess stock levels, and update your inventory list.

Test New Recipes: Provides an opportunity to try out recipes using preserved foods, helping you identify gaps in nutrition or variety and refine your meal plans.

Family Feedback: Gather feedback from family members regularly to understand their likes, dislikes, and any changes in dietary preferences.

Wrapping it Up...

Being organized with meal planning can keep your family fed and healthy during unexpected situations. The 3-Tier food storage method is a great way to have a variety of foods available, from fresh to long-lasting options. This setup makes it easy to switch between different types of food, whether it's a short-term issue or a more serious emergency. Not only does meal planning help you make the most of your food supply, but it also gives you peace of mind, knowing you're prepared for whatever may come your way.

Key Points

Meal Planning Goals: Essential for balancing nutrition, reducing food waste, and efficiently using your food storage.
Inventory: Regularly check your food inventory, using the 3-tier system to manage short-term, intermediate-term, and long-term food supplies.
Nutritional Needs: Plan meals to include a variety of macronutrients and micronutrients, incorporating superfoods for enhanced nutrition.
Caloric Needs: Determine each family member's daily caloric requirements and plan meals that meet these energy needs.
Meal Plans: Use weekly or monthly meal plans to schedule meals, ensuring variety and seasonal adjustments.
Preserved Foods: Integrate preserved foods into daily meals to maintain variety and nutritional balance.
Prep and Batch Cooking: Plan meals that can be prepped in advance and consider batch cooking to save time during the week.
Using Leftovers: Plan to use leftovers creatively to reduce waste and make meal preparation easier.
Flexibility and Variety: Be flexible with your meal plans and ensure a variety of foods to prevent menu fatigue and maintain interest in eating healthy.
Emergency Planning: Ensures a stable food supply during emergencies while maintaining nutritional balance and variety in the diet.
Emergency Meal Kit: Will sustain you if SHTF and have to grab and go.

Online Resources

- USDA FoodData Central: Detailed nutritional information for various food items. https://fdc.nal.usda.gov/

- USDA MyPlate: Information on nutrition and healthy eating. Offers a variety of tools, guidelines, and resources to help individuals and families make healthier food choices. https://www.myplate.gov/

- Centers for Disease Control and Prevention (CDC) - The CDC provides resources and guidelines on emergency preparedness, including food safety and public health concerns during disasters. https://emergency.cdc.gov/

- EatByDate: Provides information on food shelf life and tips on managing special dietary needs within a stockpile. https://eatbydate.com/

10

REAL WORLD EXAMPLES

Iceland's volcanic eruptions forced locals to rely on dried fish and stored barley for survival in the 1700s.

Planning for long-term food storage is one thing, but seeing it in action makes a difference. In this chapter, you'll find stories of families who faced unexpected challenges, like hurricanes and power outages, and how they used their prep strategies to stay safe and well-fed.

These real-life examples show how different situations impact food availability and offer practical solutions that fit various lifestyles and environments. Whether it's a rural family in the South dealing with weeks of isolation after a hurricane or a couple in the Pacific Northwest braving tough winters, these stories highlight the power of being prepared.

Through these accounts, you'll discover how key elements like meal planning, waterproof storage, and DIY food preservation can work together to build a resilient food system. More importantly, these stories prove that with a bit of foresight, anyone can turn potential crises into manageable situations.

A Midwest Storm

Mark, Sarah, and their 8-year-old daughter Emma live in a snug little house out in the Midwest countryside. Life there is pretty chill, but it's not without its hiccups, like that one winter when a nasty storm trapped them at home for nearly two weeks. The nearest grocery store was too far, and the roads were completely blocked. They ran out of food fast, and the power outage made things even trickier. Their frozen meals were spoiled without electricity, and they burned through fresh produce and dairy in just a few days. That whole experience was a real eye-opener.

Determined not to be caught off guard again, Mark and Sarah decided to revamp their food storage game. They figured out how much food their family would need to comfortably ride out emergencies, aiming for a three-month supply that balanced calories and nutrition. They weren't just looking to stockpile cans of beans; they wanted a system that fit their family's everyday needs and could handle any surprises.

First up, they diversified their food stockpile. They started loading up on long-lasting staples like rice, oats, and lentils—foods that provide solid nutrition and can last for years if stored right. Sarah got into canning, preserving tomatoes, green beans, and peaches from their summer garden. Their pantry soon filled with colorful jars of homemade goodies, alongside store-bought essentials like canned soups, meats, and powdered milk.

Meal planning turned out to be a game-changer for them. They made it a point to plan meals around what they had in the pantry, keeping things interesting so they wouldn't get bored with the same old dishes. Canned tomatoes morphed into hearty soups and pasta sauces, while dried fruits made breakfast oatmeal something Emma actually looked forward to. Even sauerkraut and pickles found their way into stir-fries and sandwiches, adding some zesty flavor.

When winter rolled around again, another storm hit. But this time, they were ready. Mark fired up their portable propane stove, and in no time, they had a warm, hearty soup made from canned veggies and beans. Thanks to their collapsible water containers and purification tablets, they didn't have to stress about running out of water either. They used what they had wisely, focusing on foods that needed little water and minimal cleanup.

The difference was incredible. Not only did the Johnsons stay cozy and well-fed, but they also had enough supplies to share with a neighbor who wasn't as prepared. They felt like that storm wasn't a crisis but a challenge they totally aced. Now, they've got peace of mind and a way of life that keeps them secure, no matter what Mother Nature throws their way.

Hurricane 'Delta'

Tom and Lisa, a couple in their middle years living in the southern U.S., were used to hurricane season. They braced themselves for the strong winds and heavy rains every year, but Hurricane Delta threw them a curveball. This storm brought some serious flooding, knocking out power and leaving them cut off from local stores for three whole weeks. Their pantry, which only had a few essentials, ran dry pretty quickly. Meals got smaller, and they had to stretch out what little food they had left. It was a wake-up call. They knew they needed a better plan for emergencies.

Once the floodwaters finally receded, Tom and Lisa jumped into action. They realized they couldn't depend on fresh food or their freezer during long power outages, so they set out to build a stash of long-lasting, non-perishable items. They started by buying bulk staples like rice, beans, and pasta, which could last long if stored correctly. Then, they quickly filled their shelves with canned goods like vegetables, fruits, soups, and proteins like tuna and chicken.

Lisa, excited to make the most of the fresh produce around them, dove into learning how to preserve food at home. She canned tomatoes, green beans, and peaches, and even pickled cucumbers and okra. Not only did this boost their stockpile, but it also added some tasty variety to their meals. Meanwhile, Tom was busy figuring out how to protect their food storage from future floods. They invested in waterproof storage bins and raised their shelves to keep everything safe from rising water.

Water was another biggie on their list. They picked up collapsible water containers and purification tablets for their emergency kit, making sure they'd have clean drinking water even if the local supply gets contaminated. To prepare for long stretches of isolation, they also whipped up a meal plan based on their stored foods. Beans and rice turned into hearty chili, canned veggies became comforting stews, and pickled okra added a zesty crunch to sandwiches.

When the next hurricane season rolled around, another powerful storm hit, bringing the same intense flooding. Once again, Tom and Lisa found themselves cut off. But this time, they were totally ready. Their waterproof storage kept everything dry, and their portable propane stove let them whip up hot meals even without power. They rotated through their stockpile, enjoying a variety of satisfying meals that kept them nourished and healthy. With their stored water, they never had to stress about staying hydrated.

Even with the extended isolation, Tom and Lisa stayed calm and well-fed. Their prep work really paid off, giving them both sustenance and peace of mind. By the time the roads reopened, they still had plenty of supplies left. This whole experience solidified their commitment to being prepared, proving that with a little planning and some waterproof storage, they could tackle even the toughest storms with confidence.

Wrapping it Up...

Preparing really brings a sense of security and calm. By mixing things like smart stockpiling, meal planning, and flexible storage options, anyone can create a solid system to keep their home running smoothly during tough times. These experiences remind us how important it is to learn from the past so we can tweak and enhance our plans for what's ahead.

11

Plan Review and Checklist

The Swiss government mandates every citizen keep at least a week's worth of food and water in case of emergencies.

F inishing your *Food Survival Plan* is a big win. It gives you the know-how and tools to tackle whatever life throws your way. By taking the time to assess your needs, organize your storage, build a balanced stockpile, and plan your meals, you've laid down a solid foundation for security and resilience. This is about filling your pantry and creating a sustainable food storage strategy that keeps your household healthy and happy.

Review and Maintain Your Plan

Creating a plan is a great accomplishment, but remember to keep it running smoothly with regular reviews and updates:

Conduct Regular Inventory Checks: Set a schedule (e.g., monthly or quarterly) to review your pantry and stockpile.

Adjust for Changing Needs: Update quantities or food types to reflect new caloric needs, preferences, or restrictions.

Monitor Storage Conditions: Check that storage areas remain cool, dry, and pest-free. Inspect containers for any damage and ensure they're adequately sealed.

Update Your Meal Plans: Refresh meal plans periodically to incorporate new foods and avoid palate fatigue. Experiment with recipes using preserved items to maintain variety and enjoyment.

Replenish and Restock: Regularly replenish items that have been used or are nearing expiration. Watch for sales or bulk purchase opportunities to keep your stockpile fully supplied.

Re-evaluate Every 6-12 Months: Periodically reassess your *Food Survival Plan*, ensuring it aligns with any lifestyle changes or new preparedness goals.

Food Survival Plan Checklist

Here is a final checklist to make sure you have everything covered. If you have ticked all the boxes, congratulations, you've got yourself a *Food Survival Plan* that ensures your household remains well-fed and secure during emergencies.

PREPPER'S FOOD SURVIVAL PLAN

Chapter	Task	Description	Status
Setting Goals & Building a Plan	Your Goals	Emergency Preparation, Self-Sufficiency, Nutrition, Cost	☐
DIY Food Preservation	DIY Preservation	Learn of the different DIY food preservation methods.	☐
Essential Foods	Download Spreadsheet	Use spreadsheet with the *Prepper's Food Survivor Calculator* and other resources to assist with your Food Survival Plan	☐
	Fill in Your DIY Food Preservation Table	Your DIY Preservation Foods.	☐
	Fill in Your Taste and Comfort Foods Table	Your preferred flavor and mood foods.	☐
	Fill in Your Essential Foods Table	Your essential foods from the five major food groups.	☐
Stockpile & Pantry	Optimize Your Storage	Store food in a cool, dry, dark environment	☐
	Waterproof Your Food Storage	Use waterproof and airtight containers.	☐
	Fill in Your Food Storage Containers Table	Use the correct recommended container to keep your essential foods fresh and safe.	☐
	Implement The 3-Tier Storage System	Use the 3-Tier Storage System (Short-term, Medium-term, Long-term)	☐
	Implement FIFO	Stock rotation method to keep foods fresh.	☐
	Consider Using Free Food App	To assist in organizing your food storage	☐
Calculating Food Storage	Example Household	Follow the steps on how to calculate food quantities for an example household.	☐
	Calculate Food Storage Quantities	Use the spreadsheet calculator to calculate your own food quantities based on your Household, Essential Foods and Storage Period.	☐
Step-by-Step Stockpile Build	Complete the 10-Step Stockpile Build	Using your essential foods quantities and lessons learned from the previous chapters	☐
Meal Planning	Fill in Your 7-Day Meal Plan Table	Create Your meal plan based on T1, T2 and T3 foods from your Essential Foods.	☐
	Fill In Your Emergency Meal Kit Table	Create Your own Emergency Meal kit	☐

Conclusion

"Preparedness is the key to success and victory." – Douglas MacArthur

As we conclude *Off The Grid Prepper's Food Survival Plan*, I hope you feel inspired to continue your journey toward food security and self-sufficiency. Whether you've already developed a comprehensive plan or are taking it one step at a time, this book serves as your trusted resource.

Remember, your journey doesn't need to be flawless or rushed. You might just be starting to think about building a stockpile, or you could be getting into DIY food preservation. No matter where you are on this path, what truly matters is making progress. Over time, you'll establish a system that suits you and your household, providing peace of mind and the confidence to tackle any challenges that come your way.

While the world can be unpredictable, your preparedness doesn't have to be. Use this guide as a handy resource whenever you need to tweak or enhance your plan. Regular check-ins, updates, and a flexible approach will keep your food survival strategy strong and ready for the long term.

Here's to a future where you're prepared, self-reliant, and well-nourished.

Appendix A

ANDREW RAINES

	Foods	Calories	Serving Size	Serving Unit
Carbs/Grains	Barley	193	1	oz
	Buckwheat	78	1	oz
	Bulgur	75	1	oz
	Corn meal	103	1	oz
	Flour	103	1	oz
	Millet	103	1	oz
	Oats	110	1	oz
	Pasta	105	1	oz
	Quinoa	106	1	oz
	Rice	102	1	oz
	Rye	80	1	oz
	Wheat	96	1	oz
Proteins	Beef Jerky	85	1	oz
	Canned Beans (DIY)	120	0.25	jar
	Canned Beef (DIY)	200	0.25	jar
	Canned Chickpeas (DIY)	120	0.25	jar
	Canned Ham (DIY)	200	0.25	jar
	Canned Meat (DIY)	75	0.25	jar
	Corned Beef (Can 12 oz)	120	2	oz
	Dried Beans	350	0.5	cup
	Dried Chicken Strips (DIY)	90	3	oz
	Dried Lamb (DIY)	110	3	oz
	Dried Pork (DIY)	120	2	oz
	Fermented Tofu	150	0.5	cup
	Freeze-Dried Beef	70	1	oz
	Freeze-Dried Chicken	100	2	oz
	Freeze-Dried Fish	95	2	oz
	Freeze-Dried Sausages	140	2	oz
	Frozen Chicken	140	3	oz
	Frozen Chicken Nuggets	140	1	cup
	Frozen Meat	200	3	oz
	Lentils	170	0.25	cup
	MRE	300	0.25	MRE

PREPPER'S FOOD SURVIVAL PLAN

	Foods	Calories	Serving Size	Serving Unit
Proteins	Peanut Butter	190	2	tbsp
	Pickled Fish (DIY)	110	0.25	jar
	Salt-Cured Pork (DIY)	210	3	oz
	Sardines (3 oz can)	100	1	can (3 oz)
	Smoked Fish (DIY)	160	2	oz
	Smoked Ribs (DIY)	160	3	oz
	Smoked Turkey (DIY)	120	4	oz
	Smoked Venison (DIY)	160	3	oz
	Spam (can 12 oz)	180	2	oz
	Tuna (3 oz can)	75	1	can (3 oz)
	Vacuum-Sealed Bacon	90	1	oz
	Vacuum-Sealed Chicken	120	3	oz
	Vacuum-Sealed Fish	150	3	oz
	Vacuum-Sealed Hot Dogs	150	2	oz
	Vacuum-Sealed Meat	220	3	oz
	Vacuum-Sealed Salami	220	2	oz
	Vacuum-Sealed Sausages	250	2	oz
Fats & Oils	Avocado Oil	124	1	tbsp
	Coconut Oil	117	1	tbsp
	Ghee (DIY)	112	1	tbsp
	Lard	115	1	tbsp
	Nuts & Seeds	160	1	oz
	Olive Oil	120	1	tbsp
	Peanut Oil	120	1	tbsp
	Sesame Oil	120	1	tbsp
	Sunflower Oil	120	1	tbsp
	Vegetable Oil	120	1	tbsp
Fruits & Vegetables	Banana Chips	150	1	oz
	Canned Fruit (DIY)	70	0.25	jar
	Canned Tomatoes (DIY)	35	0.25	jar
	Canned Vegetables (DIY)	40	0.25	jar
	Dried Fruits	140	1	oz
	Dried Vegetables	70	1	oz
	Fermented Beets (FYI)	40	0.25	jar
	Fermented Jalapeños (DIY)	10	0.25	jar
	Fermented Kimchi (DIY)	30	0.25	jar
	Freeze-Dried Fruits	110	1	oz
	Freeze-Dried Vegetables	30	1	oz
	Frozen Fruits	75	1	cup
	Frozen Vegetables	50	1	cup
	Kimchi (DIY)	20	0.25	jar
	Pickled Beets (DIY)	45	0.25	jar
	Pickled Onions (DIY)	15	0.25	jar
	Sauerkraut & Pickles	25	0.25	jar
	Smoked Eggplant (DIY)	25	3	oz
	Smoked Peppers (DIY)	20	3	oz
	Vacuum-Sealed Kale (DIY)	45	4	oz
	Vacuum-Sealed Sweet Corn	60	4	oz

ANDREW RAINES

Category	Foods	Calories	Serving Size	Serving Unit
Dairy	Evaporated Milk	40	0.25	can
	Freeze-Dried Cheese (DIY)	110	3	oz
	Powdered Milk	130	3	tbsp
	Salted Butter	100	2	oz
	Shelf-Stable Cheese	110	1	oz
	Shelf-Stable Milk	150	1	cup
	Smoked Cheese (DIY)	110	1	oz
	Vacuum-Sealed Butter	90	2	oz
Herbs & Spices	Cinnamon	6	1	tsp
	Dried Herbs	10	1	tsp
	Garlic Powder	10	1	tsp
	Onion Powder	10	1	tsp
	Salt	0	1	tsp
	Spices	10	1	tsp
Condiments & Sauces	Barbecue Sauce	70	2	tbsp
	Maple Syrup	50	1	tbsp
	Mayonnaise	90	1	tbsp
	Mustard	5	1	tbsp
	Soy, Hot sauce, Ketchup	10	1	tbsp
	Vacuum-Sealed Garlic	25	1	oz
	Vinegar	3	1	tbsp
	Worcestershire Sauce	5	1	tsp
Comfort Foods	Candied Ginger (DIY)	100	2	tbsp
	Chocolate	160	1.5	oz
	Frozen Waffles	300	1	each
	Fruit Jam (DIY)	50	1	tbsp
	Granola Bars	150	1	bar
	Instant Pudding Mix	100	1	cup
	Jarred Nutella	200	2	tbsp
	Sugared Pecans (DIY)	150	1	tbsp
	Sugared Strawberries (DIY)	120	0.25	jar
	Trail Mix	160	0.5	cup
Beverages	Coffee (Ground)	2	2	tbsp
	Fruit Juices	130	1	cup
	Hot Chocolate	150	2	tbsp
	Powdered Drink	115	2	tbsp
	Tea bags	0	1	tea bag
Other	Baking Powder, Yeast	10	1	tsp
	Honey	21	1	tsp
	Sugar	16	1	tsp
	Water	0	1	gal

www.ingramcontent.com/pod-product-compliance
Lightning Source LLC
Chambersburg PA
CBHW052136070526
44585CB00017B/1843